45A-T-ASL

Rhyming Signing

Proper Handshapes with Precise Movements for American Sign Language

Rhyming Signing

Proper Handshapes with Precise Movements for American Sign Language

BRAD WYANT

B.W. Images, Inc.
Sioux Falls, SD

Rhyming Signing: Proper Handshapes with Precise Movements for American Sign Language

Copyright © 2010 by Brad Wyant

A number of entered words that we have reason to believe constitute trademarks have been designated as such. However, no attempt has been made to designate as trademarks or service marks all terms or words in which proprietary rights might exist. The inclusion, exclusion, or definition of a word or term is not intended to affect, or to express a judgment on, the validity or legal status of the word or term as a trademark, service mark, or other proprietary term.

McDonald's ® and all references to the McDonald's Corporation are used with permission.

All rights reserved. No part of this publication may be reproduced, stored in a retrieval system, or transmitted, in any form or by any means, electronic, mechanical, photocopying, recording, or otherwise, without prior written permission from the publisher.

Graphic Design and Layout by B.W. Images, Inc. ™

ISBN 978-0-9817210-0-2
Library of Congress Control Number: 2008903492

Printed in the United States of America.
Network Printers, a division of Pronto Print, Inc. 1010 South 70th Street, Milwaukee, WI 53214.
Distribution and Marketing provided by Giordano World Entertainment. ™

CONTENTS

ACKNOWLEDGEMENTS		xiii
PREFACE Author's Notes		xv
INTRODUCTION		xix

PART I – HANDSHAPES

GUIDE TO UNDERSTANDING THE HANDSHAPES	3
THE HANDSHAPES	4

PART II – ALPHABET AND VARIOUS LETTER SIGNS

GUIDE TO RHYMING THE ALPHABET AND LETTER SIGNS		11
A	Act, Together	12
Open A	Soldier, Practice	14
B	Quiet, Attention	16
B-L	College, Book	18
B-L-1	Start, Show up	20
B-L-U	Through, File	22
C	Church, Class	24
Wide C	Rich, Boss	26
Flat C	Boy, Leader	28
C-L	English, Skill	30
D	Date, Diamond	32
E	Energy, Economy	34
F	Spirit, Preach	36
Open F	Choose, Connection	38
G	Gallaudet, Graduation	40
Curvy G	Moon, Camera	42
Wide G	Card, Zoom	44

Closed G	Write, Surprise	46
G-H	No, Paper clip	48
Curvy G-H	Ride, Limousine	50
H	Honor, Name	52
Bent H	Sit, Back out	54
H-Y	Upright, Unrighteous	56
I	Art, Idea	58
I-L-Y	Golden, Airplane	60
J	Jam, Juice	62
K	Careful, Kitchen	64
L	Turn, Laugh	66
M	McDonald's ®, Mature	68
Open M	Doctor, Memorial	70
N	Northern, Niece and Nephew	72
Open N	National, Nurse	74
O	Owl, Opportunity	76
Oval O	Teach, More	78
Wide O	Eye-popping, Clown	80
O-S	Many, Microwave	82
Wavy O	Few, Property	84
P	People, Politics	86
Q	Queen, Quality	88
R	Rocket, Research	90
R-L	Review, Retirement	92
S	Yes, Senator	94
T	Team, Tuesday	96
U	Train, Weight	98
V	Point of View, Dance	100
Bent V	Bone, Problem	102
W	Water, World	104

X	Charity, Need	106
X-A	Drum, Celebration	108
X-L	Who, Subscribe	110
X-O	Exact, Revenge	112
X-T	Remove, Champagne	114
Y	Play, Today	116
Z	Lightning, Variety	118

Part III – NUMBERS AND VARIOUS NUMERICAL SIGNS

GUIDE TO RHYMING THE NUMBERS AND NUMERICAL SIGNS		123
Zero	None, Opinion	124
Oval Zero	Expensive, Food	126
1	Think, Positive	128
Bent 1	Electricity, Cost	130
1-I	Kid, Camp	132
2	See, Voice	134
Bent 2	Tour, Ticket	136
2-K	Double, Loan	138
3	Park, Garage	140
Bent 3	Pitch, Champion	142
3-K	Triple, Third	144
4	Jail, Fence	146
Open 4	Learn, Experience	148
5	America, Trees	150
Bent 5	Tiger, Roar	152
Closed 5	Music, Appreciation	154
5-6	Five-fold, Preparatory	156
5-7	Freshman, Ring	158
5-8	Feel, Lucky	160
5-9	Nickel, Junior	162

6	Six cans, Six packages	164
7	Seven days, Seven nights	166
8	Eight Hundred, Eight Dollars	168
Open 8	Like, Message	170
8-S	Light, Pumpkin	172
9	Describe, Faith	174
Open 9	Find, Cat	176
9-S	Fox, Spot	178
10	Girl, Sport	180
Wide 10	Motor, Combine	182
11	Annual, Popcorn	184
12	Midnight, Frog	186
13	Cute, Horse	188
14	Trouble, Donkey	190
15	Better, Butterfly	192
Flat 15	Young, Advance	194
16	Sixteen weeks, Sixteen months	196
17	Seventeen thousand, Seventeen years	198
18	Eighteen million, Eighteen inches	200
19	Free, Important	202
20	Bird, Print	204
21	Gun, Shootout	206
22	Browse, Highway	208
23	Hurdle, Twenty-three times	210
24	Twenty-four hours, Twenty-four minutes	212
25	Advantage, Wait	214

REFERENCE	217
INDEX	219

If you can dream it,

you can do it.

Walt Disney

ACKNOWLEDGEMENTS

I would like to thank Professor Paul Setzer from Gallaudet University; he provided much assistance with the illustrations and encouraged me to keep going on this project. To my mother, Patricia Simmons, thank you for helping to make my labor of love a reality. B.W. Images has been immensely helpful in providing countless hours of drawing, typesetting, and research over the past five years. My special thanks to Angelo Giordano for his initial recognition of the importance of this book. To Katie Goehring, thank you for your time and help in assisting me to critique my English and the style of my writing. I would also like to recognize my family, colleagues, and friends. Your help in reading this manual and giving me your thoughtful input has allowed me to improve my book. Each of you have helped my dream to become a reality. To all of you, much thanks.

PREFACE

Author's Notes

I want to tell you a little about myself and how I got involved in this project. My first book, *You Can Sign: The Path to the Deaf Way*, focused on the manual alphabet and the numbers of American Sign Language with special attention to fingerspelling words. After that publication, I started this book using each letter and number in a complete sign. I quickly noticed there are more than just the alphabet and number handshapes. These "extra" handshapes are recognized as classifiers.

The identity of the distinctive handshapes has not been fully recognized because the research varies from one report to another on how to describe each handshape. I had to decide how to identify the handshapes. As these "extra" handshapes started to blend together over the years, a great deal of my time was spent exploring and arranging a new classification of the handshapes. We can easily overlook these classifying handshapes in this rapidly moving language, nearly hiding many of the modified letter shapes. I had to pause the sign of the word and slow down the motion to expose the additional handshapes that many people take for granted or simply skip over.

This language is all in the work of the hands. To write about sign language, a person needs to visualize the sign and create words needed to communicate that sign's idea. This process of translating American Sign Language (commonly abbreviated ASL) into English is a long and complicated one.

One day in 2004, as my friends played their guitars, the bass guitar, the drums, and the piano, I enjoyed the sounds of the music very much. I noticed the sheet music portraying all the notes used to create the different sounds. All of a sudden, I thought I can use this concept for the handshapes we so often use in ASL. I started a new project, with more extensive research, to identify the word that matched the shape of the hand. To my discovery, many handshapes had not been identified nor classified. I became interested in exactly how people sign within their everyday conversations; in the last five years, I worked to put together the writing and drawing of these previously unidentified handshapes. The process to identify the descriptions for each handshape required great patience as I researched every handshape to be as clear as possible. New challenges came with each classified handshape.

Rhyming Signing: Proper Handshapes with Precise Movements for ASL focuses on learning the distinct handshapes. This book is a wonderful tool for ASL students and teachers alike, as well as anyone who is interested in learning sign language. You will begin to learn the language by rhyming two signs and understanding the concepts of ASL. The key to understanding this language is to study and practice at your own pace. Your skills will improve as you think through and visualize using your hands to communicate instead of relying on your sense of hearing to listen and to speak vocally.

In this book, I have identified one-hundred unique handshapes. This includes the English alphabet, numbers zero through twenty-five, twenty-eight variations of the alphabet handshapes and twenty variations of the number handshapes. All of these are commonly used throughout the United States and Canada.

You will recognize how signs rhyme together visually by using the same handshape for two "rhyming" signs. Tips will be given for each sign to help you "see" the definition. Using this new approach will help you to focus on phrases that use the same handshape rather than learning only individual signs or words. This will allow you to be able to communicate in ASL very quickly.

As you know, each language has its own rules that you must follow when speaking and writing. The same is true for ASL. American Sign Language has its own unique rules regarding grammar, content and sentence structure. First, and possibly most important, in the language of ASL not all the words of a sentence are signed. Facial expressions and gestures are vitally important to understanding. These should be taught along with the sign as the two are fully integrated. For example, signing "sad" with the facial expression of a wide smile would be very confusing. The basic structure of ASL grammar is time, topic and comment. Time refers to the past, present and future tenses of any verb. Time also refers to yesterday, today or tomorrow. The topic is the subject of any sentence or phrase. Comments can be adjectives, adverbs, or any other important information added to the sentence.

For example, if you were to ask the question "Are you ready?" in ASL, the question is signed with just one sign, READY. Lowering the head, using a questioning facial expression and pointing to the other person replace the need for signing the words ARE and YOU. Answering this question with "I am ready" can be signed with just the sign READY, a smile and pointing to oneself.

Signing the phrase, "Are you ready to rhyme and sign with success?" picks out the four important words: READY, RHYME, SIGN, SUCCESS (see inside cover). "Ready" relates to time, "rhyme" and "sign" are the topics and "success" is added as a comment. The words "are," "you," "to," "and," and "with" are understood by facial expressions and gestures.

So, are you ready? Let's go!

To Your Success
Brad Wyant

INTRODUCTION

The origin of sign language, in North America, began long before European explorers discovered the New World. The Native Americans established their own sign language to converse with members of other tribes who spoke different languages. Since each tribe spoke their own language and could not understand other tribes' languages, they chose a different language to communicate. Many Native American people became very skilled in this new language that consisted of many hand signs and gestures.

As the colonial population grew, it was no surprise that they also learned this language of signs. This previously established language immensely helped the settlers to talk, work and trade with the Native Americans. Some of these early Native American signs are still used today. However, they lacked the manual alphabet system for fingerspelling words.

The origin of the manual alphabet was documented by Fray Melchor de Yebra who was a monk living in Spain. During the sixteenth century, he published drawings of the handshapes used to represent the letters of the Spanish alphabet. This new alphabet was used during Catholic brotherhoods' times of silence as well as in conversations among deaf individuals. Melchor de Yebra's drawings influenced the development of the manual alphabet now used in France, Mexico and United States. In the early seventeenth century, Juan Pablo Bonet took Melchor de Yebra's preserved hand alphabet chart and added his own concepts of deaf education. In 1620, Bonet published this information in a book titled *Simplication of the*

Letters of the Alphabet and Method of Teaching Deaf-Mutes to Speak. Bonet's work emphasized the importance of teaching deaf students to fingerspell, to work toward speaking and to read and write in the Spanish language.

In early eighteenth century, an American named Thomas Gallaudet became interested in creating a better program for deaf education in America. He and Mason Cogswell, a father of a deaf child, knew of families in New England states who had deaf children. They began searching for professors skilled in deaf education. On an extensive search, Gallaudet went to France where he found an incredibly skilled teacher named Laurent Clerc. After convincing Clerc to come to America with him, Gallaudet, Cogswell, and Clerc established the first American School for the Deaf in Hartford, Connecticut. They took the theories and ideas from French Sign Language creating what we now know as ASL.

In 1864, Edward Miner Gallaudet, the youngest child of Thomas Gallaudet, found a college for deaf students in Washington D.C. Congress and President Abraham Lincoln passed legislation to allow this new college to grant collegiate degrees. This college, now known as Gallaudet University, was the first of its kind; and it continues to offer an advanced level of deaf education today.

Some signs in ASL have not changed at all. An example is the sign for coffee; a grinding of both fists relating to grinding coffee beans. However, as time continues, ASL evolves to capture our changing society by portraying the sign in a new or different way. This is especially evident with our advancing technology and more modern designs. For example, the sign for the historic telephone used to be the first hand in the shape of a fist placed near the ear to show the receiver and the second hand, also in a fist shape, "held onto" the speaker and the base of the phone. This sign changed with our new design of the telephone. Now the sign has been simplified to using only one hand in the Y-shape with the thumb near the ear and the last finger next to the mouth.

Some signs changed due to political correction. Some foreigners who immigrated to America felt insulted and complained of stereotyping and insensitivity among deaf communities. Sliding the last finger on the side of the eye insulted the Japanese; therefore, the sign was changed to a sign showing the shape of the island. Also, people observed that some ASL signs reflected the most common religious labels of a country. For example, the sign for Italy was a cross on the forehead reflecting the Catholic customs of many Italian people. Some Italians felt offended, so the ASL sign has been changed. Today you will see people using both old and new signs throughout a conversation.

ASL is not simply English made into hand signals. ASL is truly its own language and many deaf people cherish this as their first language. ASL is not only a language of individual signs; it includes many gestures and has its own vocabulary and grammar. For example, facial expression shows how a person's mood varies during any conversation. This aspect of ASL is similar to how the tone of voice and voice inflexion portray more than just the words when used in a hearing conversation. This book shows mostly happy and some sad faces. When you ask a friend a question, that person's face may express a frown if he is confused, perplexed or misunderstanding you. If you are expecting a positive response, your facial expression would more likely be a smile. Pantomimes enrich ASL immensely, especially when talking about sporting events.

The signs of ASL have three basic parts: handshapes, positions and movements. Handshapes included in this book are the alphabet from A to Z, the numbers from zero to twenty-five and many variations of these basic handshapes. Positions include the direction the hands face (the head, the chest, the ground and others) as well as where to place the hands (near the forehead, on the arm or stomach and many more). Movements explain the hand motion from one point to another such as a spiral, an arch, up, down, or to the sides.

In general, the deaf and hard of hearing prefer to use sign language to communicate. Instead of trying to lipread and missing many of the words that are being spoken, they want to comprehend all of what is being said. Many people who are deaf use only ASL at first and then later learn to speak and to read and write in English, their second language. Many others, such as infants, people with speech development problems, children who have autism or Down's syndrome, or other speech impairments, can use sign language to communicate more clearly until their speech abilities improve. Utilizing ASL, those who are deaf or hard of hearing are able to feel more closely connected to their community; especially with families, friends, teachers, interpreters, and all the rest of the hearing population.

The spread of ASL is helping the hearing population to become more aware of Deaf culture in America. For example, several movies including "Children of a Lesser God," (1986) starring Marlee Matlin and William Hurt, and Danielle Steele's "Once in a Lifetime," (1994) starring Lindsay Wagner, encourage the hearing population to explore the complexities of the deaf person's world. As compared to ten years ago, the editors and publishers of many magazines and newspaper articles are now including much more information about ASL and deaf awareness. Sign language video logs on websites promote learning many different skills and the various complex aspects of sign language.

In the past few years, there has been significant growth and interest in learning ASL. Students can now take courses to learn ASL and earn foreign language credit. Any hearing person may meet or know someone who is deaf or hard of hearing and want to learn their language to more fully communicate with that person. Parents are learning the value of teaching sign language to their children. In this way, even infants are able to communicate their needs and wants before their speech is fully developed. Interpreters are in high demand to fulfill the growing needs of the deaf community. Some places where more interpreters are needed include public schools, video relay services, doctor offices, and within our emergency services, especially within the various medical fields. In addition, more teachers are choosing to specialize in deaf education or linguistics specifically to work with deaf children.

ASL has been adopted throughout America with varying regional signs. For example, you will see many different signs for "birthday" and "pizza." This concept of hand motion as a language has spread all over the globe. Other countries have adapted the original sign language to fit their individual cultures and needs. The same manual A-Z hand alphabet, which began centuries ago, has become standard in many countries. Just a few of these countries are Canada, Guatemala, the Philippines, Singapore, Hong Kong and several countries throughout Africa, including Cameroon and Madagascar.

Part I

HANDSHAPES

GUIDE TO UNDERSTANDING THE HANDSHAPES

When using American Sign Language (ASL), knowing and understanding the handshapes is crucial. Being familiar with the alphabetical handshapes is critical, even from the very beginning. Knowing the numerical handshapes allows you to count correctly in ASL. Some words in English simply do not have an ASL sign; those words, as well as proper names, are fingerspelled. For example, the word "rice" has no ASL sign. So when using this word the signer simply shows each letter in the word. So "rice" would be just R-I-C-E. Recognizing the variations of the most common handshapes is an integral part of learning ASL.

The drawings on the next few pages provide a useful reference table representing the most common ways to sign each handshape. It will help you to know the right handshape for the English words found in this book. This table will assist you throughout the book and in most other American Sign Language dictionaries. You should rely on this guide if you are uncertain of how to create any of the handshapes. Also, review the index if you are looking for a specific word or phrase.

THE HANDSHAPES

A	**Open A**	**B**	**B-L**	**B-L-1**	**B-L-U**	**C**
Act	Soldier	Quiet	College	Start	File	Church
Together	Practice	Attention	Book	Show up	Through	Class

Wide C	**Flat C**	**C-L**	**D**	**E**	**F**	**Open F**
Rich	Boy	English	Date	Energy	Spirit	Choose
Boss	Leader	Skill	Diamond	Economy	Preach	Connection

      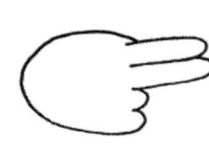

G	**Curvy G**	**Wide G**	**Closed G**	**G-H**	**Curvy G-H**	**H**
Gallaudet	Moon	Card	Write	No	Ride	Honor
Graduation	Camera	Zoom	Surprise	Paper clip	Limousine	Name

Bent H	**H-Y**	**I**	**I-L-Y**	**J**	**K**	**L**
Sit	Upright	Art	Gold	Jam	Careful	Turn
Back out	Unrighteous	Idea	Airplane	Juice	Kitchen	Laugh

M	**Open M**	**N**	**Open N**	**O**	**Oval O**
McDonald's ®	Doctor	North	National	Owl	Teach
Mature	Memorial	Niece & Nephew	Nurse	Opportunity	More

Wide O	**O-S**	**Wavy O**	**P**	**Q**	**R**
Eye-Popping	Many	Few	People	Queer	Rocket
Clown	Microwave	Property	Politics	Quality	Research

R-L	**S**	**T**	**U**	**V**	**Bent V**	**W**
Review	Yes	Team	Train	Point of View	Bone	Water
Retirement	Senator	Tuesday	Weight	Dance	Problem	World

X	**X-A**	**X-L**	**X-O**	**X-T**	**Y**	**Z**
Donate	Drum	Who	Exact	Remove	Play	Lightning
Need	Celebration	Subscribe	Revenge	Champagne	Today	Variety

Zero None Opinion	**Oval Zero** Expensive Food	**1** Think Positive	**Bent 1** Electricity Cost	**1-I** Kid Camp	**2** See Voice	**Bent 2** Tour Ticket

2-K Double Loan	**3** Park Garage	**Bent 3** Pitch Champion	**3-K** Triple Third	**4** Jail Fence	**Open 4** Learn Experience

5 America Trees	**Bent 5** Tiger Roar	**Closed 5** Music Appreciation	**5-6** Five-fold Preparatory	**5-7** Freshman Ring Finger	**5-8** Feel Lucky

5-9 Nickel Junior	**6** Six cans Six packages	**7** Seven days Seven nights	**8** Eight hundred Eight dollars	**Open 8** Like Message	**8-S** Light Pumpkin

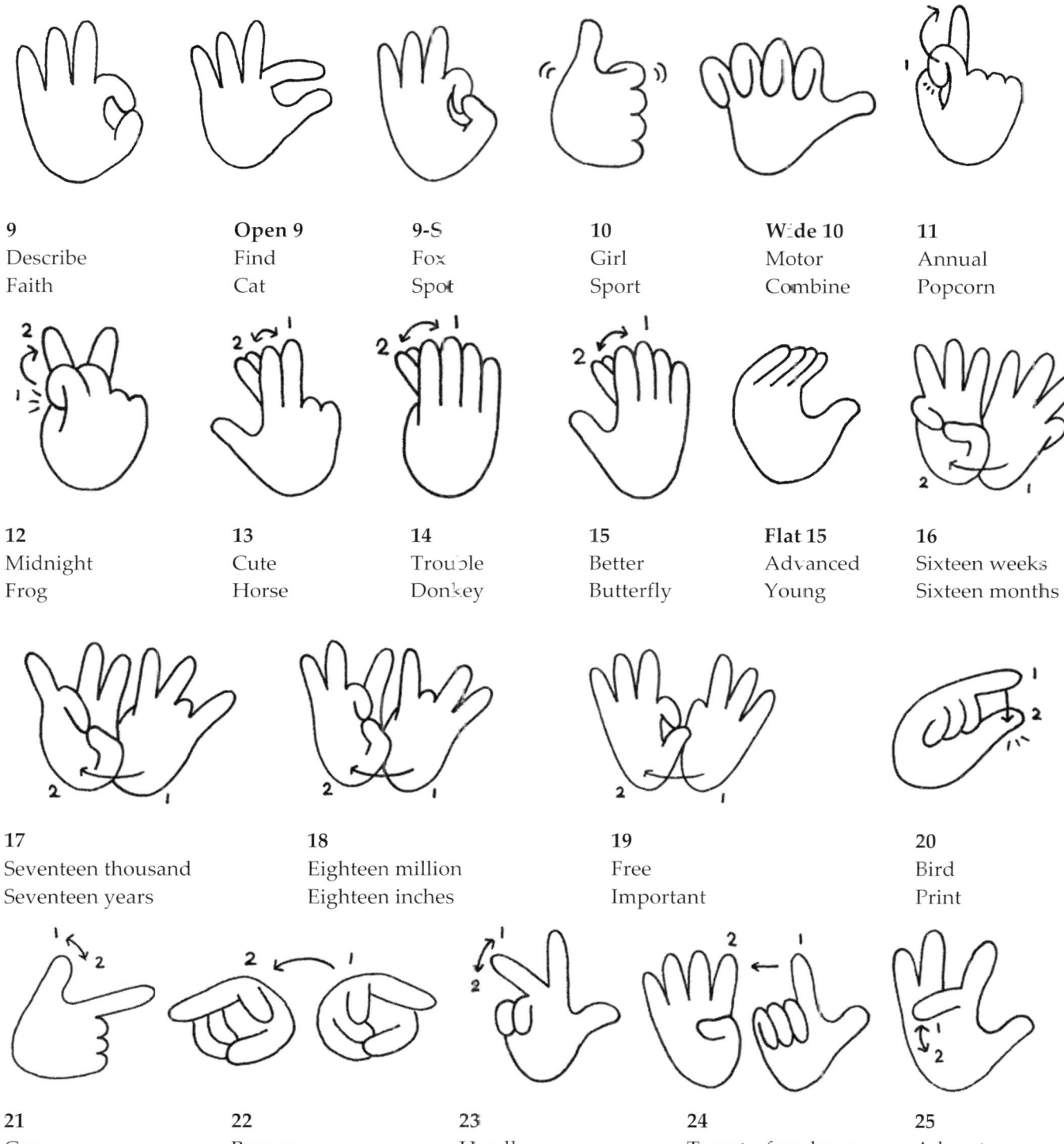

9	**Open 9**	**9-S**	**10**	**Wide 10**	**11**
Describe	Find	Fox	Girl	Motor	Annual
Faith	Cat	Spot	Sport	Combine	Popcorn
12	**13**	**14**	**15**	**Flat 15**	**16**
Midnight	Cute	Trouble	Better	Advanced	Sixteen weeks
Frog	Horse	Donkey	Butterfly	Young	Sixteen months
17	**18**	**19**		**20**	
Seventeen thousand	Eighteen million	Free		Bird	
Seventeen years	Eighteen inches	Important		Print	
21	**22**	**23**	**24**	**25**	
Gun	Browse	Hurdle	Twenty-four hours	Advantage	
Shootout	Highway	Twenty-three times	Twenty-four minutes	Wait	

Part II

ALPHABET & VARIOUS LETTER SIGNS

GUIDE TO RHYMING THE ALPHABET AND LETTER SIGNS

If you witness someone signing words to a song, you realize that music is much more than sound. The process of hand movements is an art form of its own, whether there is sound to hear or not. In the hearing world, it is easy to understand rhyming words. Young students learn quickly that while rhyming words sound alike, they have different meanings. Now, in the deaf world, imagine how hand formations can rhyme without sound. As in English, these rhyming signs do not have the same meaning.

Listening to the words "girl" and "swirl" or "boy" and "joy" you hear how the words rhyme but you know that they have different meanings. By using the concept of rhyme, the challenge of learning or memorizing American Sign Language has just become easier. When you visualizing the signs for "eye-popping" and "clown" or "people" and "politics," you will see how the signs rhyme by using the same handshape and realize simultaneously that each sign has a different meaning.

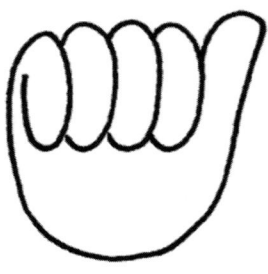 The hand creates **A** as the last four fingers fold down to the palm while the thumb is placed by the first finger.

Visualize the word **ACT** as showing two people performing their moves. Both hands take the shape of A with the thumbs facing the chest, palms facing each other. Alternate both hands in a circular motion. The motion is repeated several times.

Sign Synonyms: drama, performance, show, skit, theater

A

Using the A handshape also signs the word **TOGETHER**.

Both hands take the shape of A with the thumbs facing the chest, palms facing each other. Touch both hands to each other. Do you see the hands coming **TOGETHER**?

Sign Synonyms: altogether, with

 The hand creates the shape of the **Open A** as the thumb points apart from the fingers while the last four fingers fold down to the palm.

Visualize the word **SOLDIER** as a person holding a rifle.

Both hands take the shape of Open A with the first hand on top of the second hand, palms facing the body. Tap both hands on one side of the chest twice.

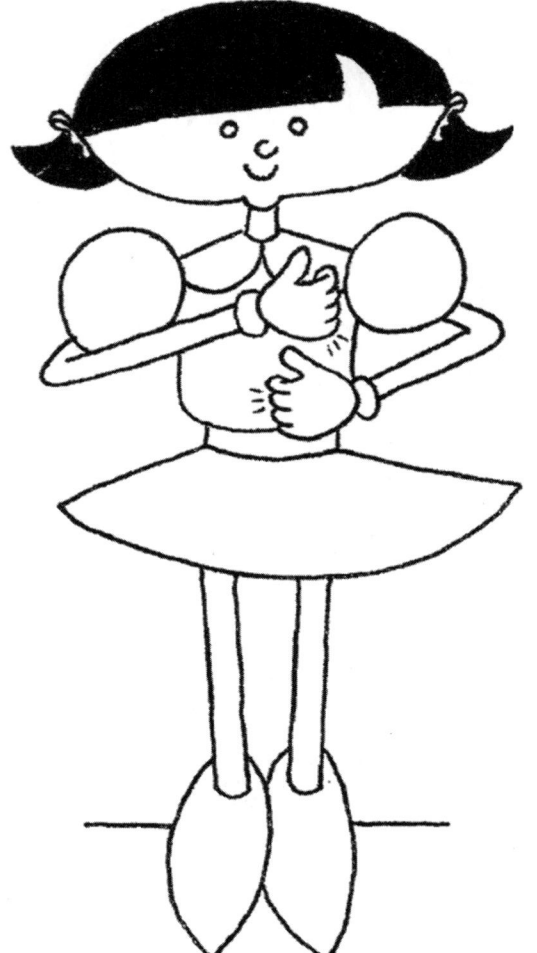

Sign Synonyms: army, combat, military

Open A

Using the Open A handshape also signs the word **PRACTICE** by using a repetitive motion. The first hand takes the shape of Open A placing the palm onto the first finger of the second hand that takes the shape of 1* with the palm facing down. Slide the first hand back and forth across the first finger of the second hand. Repeat the motion. **PRACTICE** makes perfect!

* See The Handshapes, p. 4 - 7.

Sign Synonyms: rehearsal, training

 The hand creates the shape of **B** as the last four fingers point up together while the thumb bends on the palm.

Visualize the word **QUIET** by keeping the voice hushed.

Both hands take the shape of B. Place the first hand on the lip and the first finger of the second hand on the last finger of the first hand, palms facing the side. Shift both hands downward in a semi-circular motion while the hands are apart.

Sign Synonyms & Phrase: calm, calm down, passive, silence, silent, still, tranquil

B

Using the B handshape also signs the word **ATTENTION** as keeping the eyes focused. Both hands take the shape of B. Place the hands on the side of the eyes with the palms facing each other. Shift both hands outward and back a few times.

Sign Synonym Phrase: pay attention

 The hand creates **B-L** as the four fingers point up together while the thumb points out and apart.

Visualize the word **COLLEGE** as the place of higher education.

Both hands take the shape of B-L. The palm of the first hand lies on top of the palm of the second hand. Raise the first hand in the semi-circular motion above the second hand.

Sign Synonym: collegiate

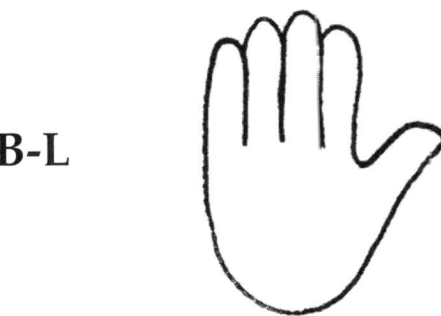

B-L

Using the B-L handshape also signs the word **BOOK** as if opening the cover of a book. Both hands take the shape of B-L and place the palms together. Both hands open in an arc, palms facing the body leaving the last finger of both hands touching. Can you read the **BOOK**?

Sign Synonyms: album, booklet, books, textbook

The hand creates **B-L-1** as the four fingers point up together and the thumb points out and apart. Then the first finger and the second finger split apart.

Visualize the word **START** as inserting a key in the ignition.

The first hand takes the shape of 1* and the second hand creates the shape of B-L-1. Point the first finger of the first hand between the first and second finger of the second hand, palms facing the body. Rotate the first hand once keeping that hands touching.

*See The Handshapes, p. 4 - 7.

Sign Synonyms: begin, origin, restart

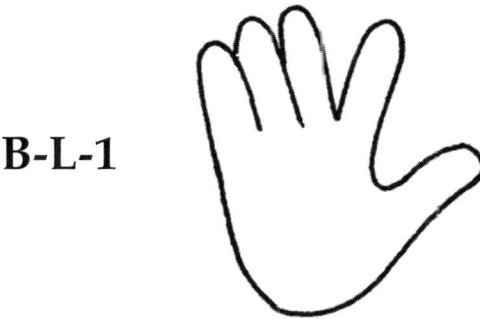

B-L-1

Using the B-L-1 handshape also signs the phrase to **SHOW UP** as if appearing from under the surface. The first hand takes the shape of 1* and is placed under the second hand that takes the shape of B-L-1 with the palm down. Move the first hand up inserting the first finger of the first hand between the first and second finger of the second hand.

*See The Handshapes, p. 4 – 7.

Sign Synonyms & Phrases: appear, incident, materialize, occur, pop up, surface, turn up

The hand creates **B-L-U** as all four fingers point up together. Then split the second and third fingers and the thumb points out and apart.

Visualize the word **FILE** as inserting the paper in the files.

The first hand takes the shape of B and the second hand creates the shape of B-L-U. Place the second hand in front of the body with the palm facing the side. Intersect the first hand between the second and third finger of the second hand. Tap the first hand once between the fingers of the second hand.

Sign Synonym: sort

B-L-U

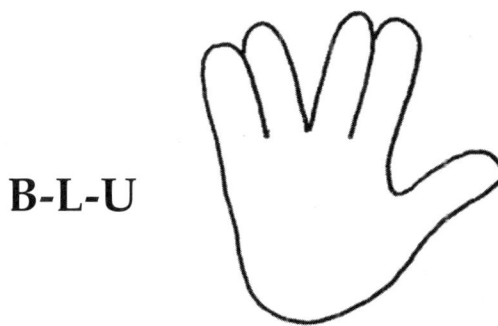

Using the B-L-U handshape also signs the word **THROUGH** as to go through a narrow passage. The first hand takes the shape of B-L and the second hand creates the shape of B-L-U with palm facing the body. Intersect the first hand between the second and third finger of the second hand with the palm facing to the side. Slide through the first hand between the fingers of the second hand.

Sign Synonym: via

The hand creates **C** as all four fingers curve while the thumb curves and facing the fingers.

Visualize the word **CHURCH** as an establishment.

The first hand takes the shape of C and is placed on the second hand that uses the shape of B-L, palm facing down. Move the first hand up and down a few times.

Sign Synonym: chapel

C

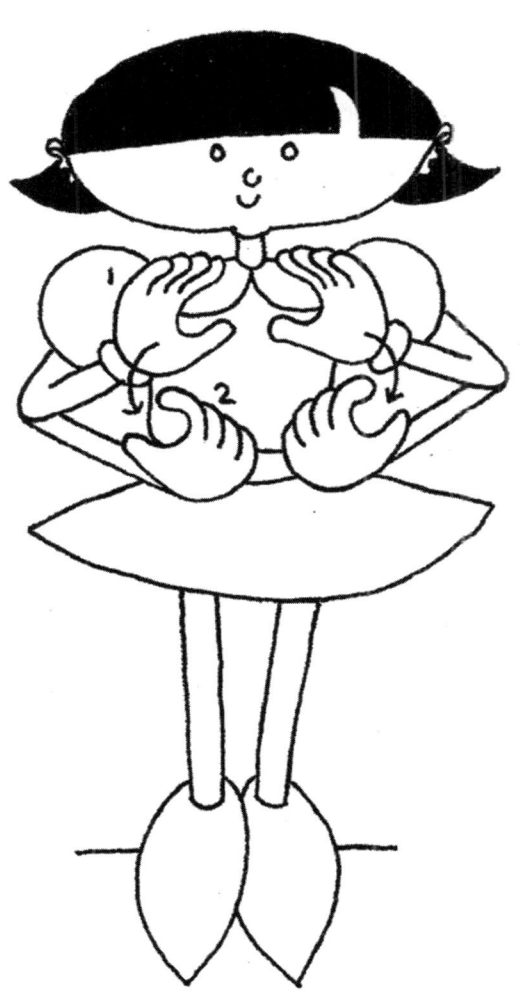

Using the C handshape also signs the word **CLASS** as if showing a group of students in their classroom.

Place both hands comfortably in front of the body using the C handshape. Start with the palms facing each other. Twist the wrists in a semi-circular motion; stop when both palms face the body.

Sign Synonyms & Phrase: bracket(s), category, classify, a group of, section, series

 The hand creates **Wide C** as all four fingers and the thumb curve and separate from each other.

Visualize the word **RICH** as expanding a stack of supplies.

The first hand takes the shape of Wide C and the tips of the fingers touch the palm of the second hand that creates the shape of 5*, palm facing up. Raise the first hand above the second hand.

*See The Handshapes, p. 4 - 7.

Sign Synonyms: fortune, jackpot, treasure, wealth

Wide C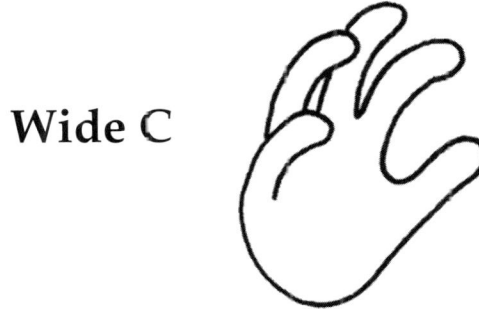

Using the Wide C handshape also signs the word **BOSS** by visualizing the decorations at the shoulder of an army general's uniform. The hand takes the shape of Wide C tapping the fingers and the thumb on the shoulder.

Sign Synonyms: captain, chief, general, officer

 The hand creates **Flat C** as all the fingers point out together while the thumb is parallel with the fingers.

Visualize the word **BOY** as a male wearing a cap.

The hand takes the shape of Flat C placing the first finger on the forehead. Tap the fingers and the thumb together, as if touching the bill of the cap.

Flat C

Using the Flat C handshape also signs the word **LEADER** as someone holding your hand and leading you away.

The first hand takes the shape of Flat C and the second hand creates the shape of B-L, palm facing the chest. The first hand holds the fingers of the second hand and pulls the second hand sideways.

Sign Synonyms: guidance, guide, lead

 The hand creates **C-L** as all the fingers curve out together while the thumb points out.

Visualize the word **ENGLISH** as hands resting on an umbrella. Both hands take the shape of C-L. The palm of the first hand is on top of the second hand with both palms facing down. Extend both hands forward and back a few times.

NOTE: This sign is for the word **ENGLISH** meaning the language of English, not England or people from England.

C-L

Using the C-L handshape also signs the word **SKILL** as if taking and applying what you have learned.

The first hand takes the shape of C-L with the palm facing the body. The second hand takes the shape of B-L with all four fingers pointing up and the palm facing the side. Grasp the second hand with the fingers of the first hand so that both palms touching each other. Slide the first hand forward and away from the second hand while changing the first hand to the handshape Open A.

Sign Synonyms: ability, able, adept, agile, capable, efficient, enable, expert, handy, proficient, skilled, talent

The hand creates the shape of **D** as the first finger points up while the last three fingers curve in and touch the thumb.

Visualize the word **DATE** as bringing two people together.

Both hands take the shape D and the palms of both hands face each other. Tap the fingers of both hands to each other a few times.

Sign Synonyms & Phrase: dating, dessert, going out with

D

Using the D handshape also signs the word **DIAMOND** as the stone in an engagement ring or other jewelry.

The first hand takes the shape of D and the second hand takes the shape of 5*, palm facing down. Tap the last three fingers of the first hand onto the third finger of the second hand a few times.

*See The Handshapes, p. 4 - 7.

 The hand creates the shape of **E** as all four fingers fold down to the palm with the thumb bent underneath the fingers.

Visualize the word **ENERGY** as a bulging bicep muscle.

The first hand takes the shape of E and is placed with the palm facing sideways on the upper bicep of the opposite arm. Rotate the first hand down in a circular motion touching the last finger onto the lower arm.

Sign Synonym: energetic

E

Using the E handshape also signs the word **ECONOMY** as holding money with one hand. The first hand takes the shape of E while the second hand takes the shape of B-L. With both palms facing up, the first hand is laid on the palm of the second hand. Tap the first hand up and down on the second hand a few times.

Sign Synonym: economic

 The hand creates the shape of **F** as the first finger touches the thumb with the last three fingers pointing up and apart.

Using the F handshape also signs the word **SPIRIT** as taking up the soul from the body. Both hands take the shape of F. The palm of the first hand faces down while the second hand faces the side. Insert the finger and the thumb of the first hand in the second hand enclosure consisting of the first finger and thumb. Move the first hand up in a wavy line and away from the second hand.

Sign Synonyms: ghost, Holy Spirit, spiritual

F

Using the F handshape also signs the word **PREACH** as if you are listening to a speech. The first hand takes the shape of F with the palm facing the front. Place your hand a bit above your shoulder and to the side. Move the hand at the wrist in a short forward and backward motion. Repeat this motion a few times. Does he **PREACH** about the **SPIRIT**?

Sign Synonym: pastor

 The hand creates the shape of **Open F** as the first finger is parallel with the thumb with the last three fingers pointing up and apart.

Visualize the word **CHOOSE** as picking from an assortment.

The first hand takes the shape of Open F and the second hand takes the shape of 5.* Place the first finger and the thumb of the first hand on the first finger of the second hand, palm facing the side. Move the first hand backward and away from the second hand while changing the shape to F.

Sign Synonyms & Phrase: choice, select, to pick one

Open F

Using the Open F handshape also signs the word **CONNECTION** as fitting together.

Both hands take the shape of Open F and the palms face each other. Move both hands inward changing both hands to the shape of F, and interlocking the fingers and thumbs.

Sign Synonyms: attach, attachment, belong, bind, bond, connect, unite

 The hand creates the shape of **G** as the first finger is parallel with the thumb while the last three fingers fold down to the palm.

Visualize the word **GALLAUDET** as seeing the glasses worn by Thomas Gallaudet, founder of the university on the campus in Washington D.C.

The hand takes the shape of G placing the finger and the thumb on one eye with the palm facing the side. Slide the hand away from the face while changing the shape to Closed G.*

*See The Handshapes, p. 4 – 7.

Sign Synonym Phrase: Gallaudet University

G

Using the G handshape also signs the word **GRADUATION** as receiving a stamp of approval from the school.

The first hand takes the shape of G with the palm facing down and the second hand takes the shape of B-L palm facing up. Place the first hand above the second hand. Twist the hand at the wrist to palm facing the side and bring down to land on the palm of the second hand.

Sign Synonym: guarantee

 The hand creates the shape of **Curvy G** as the first finger and the thumb curve while the last three fingers fold down to the palm.

Visualize the word **MOON** as looking at a sliver of the moon.

The hand takes the shape of Curvy G with the palm facing the side. Place the thumb on the side of the forehead, tapping the thumb to the forehead a few times.

Curvy G

Using the Curvy G handshape also signs the word **CAMERA** as taking a picture with a push of a button.

Both hands take the shape of Curvy G and are placed near the eyes with the palms facing each other. Wiggle the first finger of the first hand and smile.

Sign Synonyms: photograph, photography, snapshot

The hand creates the shape of **Wide G** as the first finger is parallel with the thumb while the last three fingers fold down to the palm. Then move the first finger up a little bit.

Visualize the word **CARD** as a greeting card. Both hands take the shape of Wide G and the palms face each other. The first fingers and the thumbs of both hands touch each other. Shift both hands apart. Then change the shape of both hands to Closed G.*

*See The Handshapes, p. 4 – 7.

Sign Synonyms: check, coupon, envelope

Wide G

Using the Wide G handshape also signs the word **ZOOM** as speeding away into the distance.

The first hand takes the shape of Wide G and the second hand takes the shape of 1* with the palm facing down. Place the thumb of the first hand on the bottom of the first finger of the second hand. Slide the thumb of the first hand across the first finger to the tip while changing the shape to Closed G.*

*See The Handshapes, p. 4 – 7.

Sign Synonym Phrase: start off

 The hand creates the shape of **Closed G** as the first finger touches the thumb while the last three fingers fold down to the palm.

Visualize the word **WRITE** as using a pencil on a piece of paper.

The first hand takes the shape of Closed G, the palm facing the front, and the second hand takes the shape of B-L with the palm facing the body. Place the first finger and the thumb of the first hand on the palm of the second hand. Slide the first hand across the second hand ending on the tips of the fingers.

Sign Synonyms: composition, edit

Closed G

Using the Closed G handshape also signs the word **SURPRISE** as the facial expression of the eyes widening.

Both hands take the shape of Closed G with the palms facing each other. Touch the first finger and the thumb to the side of each eye. Move the hands upward while changing the shape to Wide G. Open eyes wide at the same time.

Sign Synonyms: amaze, amazement, astound, bewildered, shock, startle

 The hand creates the shape of **G-H** as the first two fingers point out together and the thumb is parallel with the first two fingers while the last two fingers fold down to the palm.

Visualize the word **NO** as closing the mouth. The first hand takes the shape of G-H with the palm facing the front. Snap the first two fingers down onto the thumb.

Sign Synonym & Phrase: no way, nope

G-H

Using the G-H handshape also signs the word **PAPER CLIP** as if attaching some papers together.

The first hand takes the shape of G-H and the second hand takes the shape of B with the palm facing the body. Place the thumb of the first hand on the palm of the second hand. Touch the first two fingers to the back of the second hand.

 The hand creates the shape of **Curvy G-H** as the first two fingers curve and the thumb points parallel to the first two fingers while the third and fourth fingers fold down to the palm.

Visualize the word **RIDE** as if you are miming a person getting into a vehicle and driving away.

The first hand takes the shape of Curvy G-H with the palm facing up. The second hand takes the shape of C with the palm facing to the side. Twist the wrist of the first hand until the palm faces down. The first hand's first two fingers will land on the thumb of the second hand. Then move both hands forward a few inches.

Sign Synonym & Phrase: riding, to ride with

Curvy G-H

Using the Curvy G-H handshape also signs the word **LIMOUSINE** as a stretched car. Both hands take the shape of Curvy G-H placing the first hand behind the second hand, palms facing each other. Move the first hand straight back and away from the second hand. Do you want to **RIDE** in the **LIMOUSINE** with us?

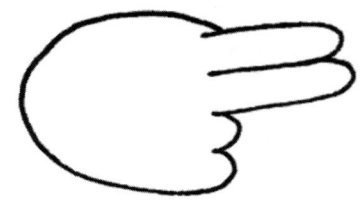 The hand creates the shape of **H** as the first two fingers point out together while the last two fingers fold down to the palm with the thumb resting on the third finger.

Visualize the word **HONOR** as showing your respect for a person who has a higher position than you.

Both hands take the shape of H with the palms facing each other. Place the first hand's first finger on the forehead with the fingers pointing up. Then place the second hand out in front of the body, slightly lower than the first hand, but also with the fingers pointing up. Move both hands forward and up as in an upside-down arch; ending with both hands above the head. Do you **HONOR** your parents?

Sign Synonyms: highness, honorable

H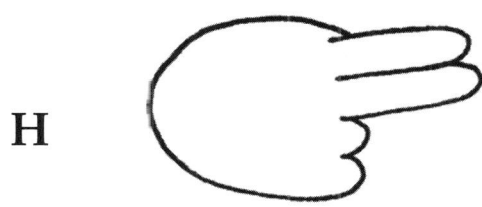

Using the H handshape also signs the word **NAME**; this is most often used when you introduce yourself.

Both hands take the shape of H with the palms facing the body. Place the first hand a bit above the second hand at a perpendicular angle. Your hands will form an "X" shape. Tap the second finger of the first hand on the first finger of the second hand two times.

Sign Synonym and Phrase: nominee, is called

The hand creates the shape of **Bent H** as the first two fingers point out together while the last two fingers fold down to the palm with the thumb resting on the third finger. Then bend the first two fingers down a bit.

Visualize the word **SIT** as someone sitting on the chair.

The first hand takes the shape of Bent H and the second hand takes the shape of H with both palms facing down. Place the first hand above the second hand. Move the first hand down landing on the first two fingers of the second hand.

Sign Synonym Phrase: sit down

Bent H

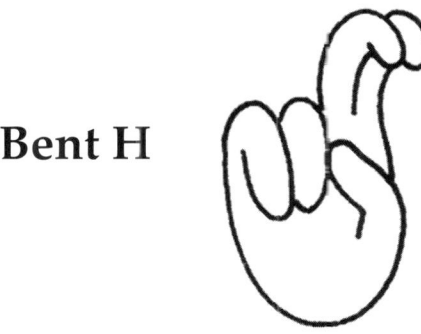

Using the Bent H handshape also signs the phrase to **BACK OUT** as leaving the group. The first hand takes the shape of Bent H with the palm facing down. The second hand takes the shape of O* with the palm facing the side. Insert the first two fingers of the first hand into the circle made by the second hand. Withdraw the first hand out, up and back, from the second hand.

*See The Handshapes, p. 4 – 7.

Sign Synonyms & Phrases: draw back, drop out, quit, resign

 The hand creates the shape of **H-Y** as the first two fingers point up together and the third finger bends down while the last finger and the thumb point out and apart.

Visualize the word **UPRIGHT** as if someone is raising the standards to a higher level. The first hand takes the shape of H-Y near the shoulder with the palm facing the front. Raise the hand back a little bit.

Sign Synonyms & Phrase: devout, holy, in good standing, pious, righteous

H-Y

Using the H-Y handshape also signs the word **UNRIGHTEOUS** showing a person of low esteem.

The first hand takes the shape of H-Y with the palm facing the front near the shoulder. Move the forearm down at the elbow so that the palm is facing down.

Sign Synonym & Phrase: unholiness, not following the rules

 The hand creates the shape of **I** as the last finger points up while the first three fingers fold down to the palm with the thumb resting across the first finger.

Visualize the word **ART** as painting on a canvas.

The first hand takes the shape of I and the second hand takes the shape of B-L with the palm facing the body. Lay the last finger of the first hand on the palm of the second hand. Slide the first hand down in a wavy movement stopping on the bottom of the second hand.

Sign Synonyms: drawing, illustration, sketch

I

Using the I handshape also signs the word **IDEA** as a thought coming out of your head. The first hand takes the shape of I with the palm facing the head. Touch the last finger on the side of the forehead. Move the hand forward and away from the head. Open the eyes wide at the same time.

Sign Synonym Phrases: I have an idea, new idea

The hand creates the shape of **I-L-Y** as the first finger points up and the second and third finger fold down to the palm. The last finger and the thumb point out and apart.

Visualize the word **GOLDEN** as showing off a shiny earring.

The first hand takes the shape of I-L-Y with the palm facing the head. Place the first finger on the ear. Slide the hand forward changing to the handshape Y.*

Then rotate the Y shape side to side at the wrist.

*See The Handshapes, p. 4 – 7.

Sign Synonyms: California, gold

I-L-Y

Using the I-L-Y handshape also signs the word **AIRPLANE** by resembling a plane taking off into the air.

The first hand takes the shape of I-L-Y with the palm facing down. Move the hand forward and back a few times.

Sign Synonyms: airline, airport, jet, plane

The hand creates the shape of **J** as the last finger points up while the first three fingers fold down to the palm with the thumb resting across the first finger. Then the last finger makes an "imaginary line" similar to the letter J, ending with the palm facing the side.

Visualize the word **JAM** as spreading a piece of bread with jam.

The first hand takes the shape of J palm facing down; the second hand takes the shape of B-L with the palm facing up. Place the first hand above the second hand. Rotate the first hand in the "J" motion, sliding the last finger on the second hand's palm.

Sign Synonym: jelly

J

Using the J handshape also signs the word **JUICE** as the taste of the beverage.

The first hand takes the shape of J with the palm facing the head. Start with the last finger at the end of the mouth. Sign **JUICE** by touching the last finger against the cheek while moving the wrist in the "J" motion.

 The hand creates the shape of **K** as the first finger points up and the second finger points up diagonally with the thumb resting on the lower joint of the second finger. The last two fingers fold down to the palm.

Visualize the word **CAREFUL** as putting two things together gently.

Both hands take the shape of K with the palms facing each other. Place the first hand above the second hand. Tap the first hand on the second hand a few times.

Sign Synonym & Phrases: be careful, cautious, take care

K

Using the K handshape also signs the word **KITCHEN** as if you are miming flipping over a pancake with a spatula.

The first hand takes the shape of K with the palm facing down. The second hand takes the shape of B-L with the palm facing up. Place the first hand on the palm of the second hand. Twist the wrist of the first hand away from the body causing the K handshape to flip over. End with the first hand's palm facing up. Do you smell the **FOOD** in the **KITCHEN**?

 The hand creates the shape of **L** as the first finger and the thumb point out and apart while the last three fingers fold down to the palm.

Visualize the word **TURN** as showing the order of who is next.

The first hand takes the shape of L with the palm facing the body. Rotate the hand in a forward arching motion; stop when the palm is facing up.

Sign Synonyms: alternate, next

L

Using the L handshape also signs the word **LAUGH** in a motion resembling a smile. Both hands take the shape of L with the palms facing the head. Place the first fingers of both hands on the side of each cheek. Stroke the first fingers sideways on the cheek in a small circular motion a few times.

Sign Synonyms: chuckle, giggle, laughing, laughter

 The hand creates the shape of **M** as all four fingers fold down to the palm.

The thumb is then inserted between the third and fourth finger.

Visualize the word **MCDONALD'S** ® seeing the large golden arches in the restaurant's sign.

The first hand takes the shape of M and the second hand takes the shape of B-L with both palms facing down. Place the first hand on top of the second hand. Move the first hand up in an arching motion while changing the handshape to D. Then bring the first hand in the D handshape, down to touch the back of the second hand.

M

Using the M handshape also signs the word **MATURE** as if a person is growing up. The first hand takes the shape of M with the palm facing the front and the second hand takes the shape of B-L with the palm facing the side. Place the side of the first hand on the palm of the second hand. Slide the first hand up until it reaches the tips of the fingers of the second hand.

Sign Synonyms: maturity, morals

 The hand creates the shape of **Open M** as all the fingers fold down to the palm and the thumb is inserted between the third and fourth finger. Then raise the first three fingers up a bit.

Visualize the word **DOCTOR** as if someone is feeling the pulse on the wrist. The first hand takes the shape of Open M with the palm facing down and the second hand takes the shape of B-L with the palm facing up. Place the fingertips of the first hand above the wrist of the second hand. Tap the first three fingers on the wrist of the second hand a few times.

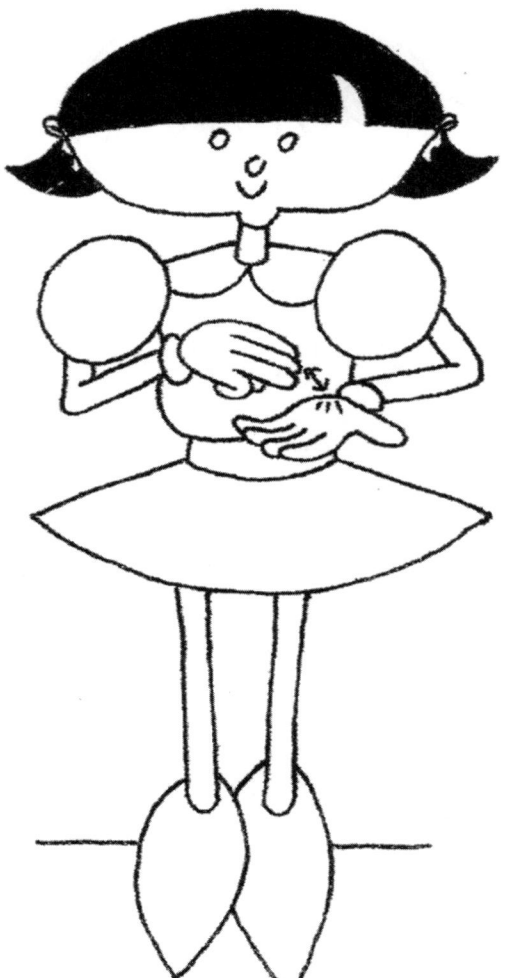

Sign Synonym & Phrase: medical doctor, physician

Open M

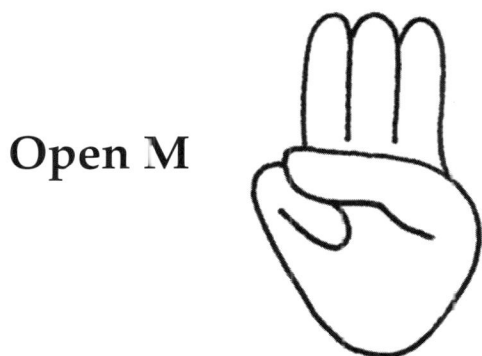

Using the Open M handshape also signs the word **MEMORIAL** as if a group is putting up a plaque to remember someone.

The first hand takes the shape of Open M with the palm facing the head. Place the first three fingertips on the forehead. Then remove the fingertips and push the hand back at the side of the head.

Sign Synonym & Phrase: memorable, Memorial Day

 The hand creates the shape of **N** as all four fingers fold down to the palm and the thumb is inserted between the second and third finger.

Visualize the word **NORTH** as the arrow pointing up on a compass.

The first hand takes the shape of N and is placed in front of the chest with the palm facing the side. Move the hand straight up a little bit.

Sign Synonym: northern

N

Using the N handshape also signs the words **NIECE** and **NEPHEW** placed at the cheek for females and the forehead for males. The first hand takes the shape of N with the palm facing the side. To sign the word **NIECE**, place the hand near the cheek and twist the wrist back and forth a few times. Use the same handshape and wrist motion to sign the word **NEPHEW**. The only change needed is to place the N handshape near the forehead instead of the cheek.

 The hand creates the shape of **Open N** as all the fingers fold down to the palm and the thumb is inserted between the second and the third finger. Then raise the first two fingers up a bit.

Visualize the word **NATIONAL** as a whole land.

The first hand takes the shape of Open N and the second hand takes the shape of B-L with both palms facing down. Place the first hand above the second hand. Move the first hand in a small circular motion, then end by moving down and landing on the back of the second hand.

Sign Synonyms and Phrase: nation, natural, nature, normal, of course

Open N

Using the Open N handshape also signs the word **NURSE** as if someone is feeling the pulse on the wrist.

The first hand takes the shape of Open N with the palm facing down and the second hand takes the shape of B-L with the palm facing up. Place the fingertips of the first hand above the wrist of the second hand. Tap the first two fingers on the wrist of the second hand a few times. You're right! It is very close to the sign for **DOCTOR**.

Sign Synonym: nursing

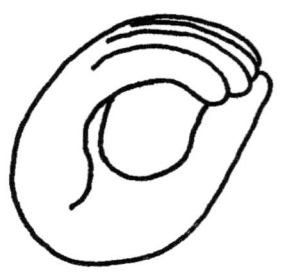 The hand creates the shape of **O** as the first four fingers curve and the thumb touches the curved fingers.

Visualize the word **OWL** as a bird looking with two big eyes.

Both hands take the shape of O with the palms facing each other. Place the side of both hands on the eyes. Rotate the wrist back and forth a few times, as if trying to focus or see the bird.

Sign Synonyms: binoculars, owlet

O

Using the O handshape also signs the word **OPPORTUNITY** as if someone is opening a way to move forward

Both hands take the shape of O with both palms facing down. Place the hands near the upper stomach with the elbows at the sides. Push both hands forward while changing both hands to the handshape P.*

*See The Handshapes, p. 4 – 7.

 The hand creates the shape of **Oval O** as the first four fingers curve and the thumb touches the curved fingers. Then flatten out the fingers and the thumb.

Visualize the word **TEACH** as giving new information to others, increasing their knowledge.

Both hands take the shape of Oval O with the palms facing each other. Place the hands near each side of the forehead. Shake both hands forward and back a few times.

Sign Synonyms: educate, education, indoctrinate, indoctrination, instruct, instruction

Oval O

Using the Oval O handshape also signs the word **MORE** as if adding extra to what you already have.

Both hands take the shape of Oval O with the palms facing each other. Place both hands side by side in front of the body. Tap the fingertips and the thumbs of both hands together a few times.

 Begin the **Wide O** with the O handshape. Then expand all the fingers and the thumb out a little bit.

Visualize the phrase **EYE-POPPING** as if just learning something very surprising. Both hands take the shape of Wide O with the palms facing the head. Place each hand over the eye and close the eyes. Move both hands forward. Open both eyes and the mouth wide at the same time.

Wide O

Using the Wide O handshape also signs the word **CLOWN** visualizing the typical big red nose.

The first hand takes the shape of Wide O with the palm facing the head. Place the tips of the fingers and thumb on the nose. Wiggle the hand and smile.

The hand creates the shape of **O-S** as the first four fingers curve together and the thumb overlaps the fingertips.

Visualize the word **MANY** as the hand is full and making more.

Both hands take the shape of O-S with the palms facing up. Place both hands side by side in front of the body. Change both hands to the shape 5.*

*See The Handshapes, p. 4 – 7.

Sign Synonyms & Phrase: a lot, lots, multitude, numerous

O-S

Using the O-S handshape also signs the word **MICROWAVE** as resembling the beam waves inside the appliance.

Both hands take the shape of O-S with the palms facing each other. Place both hands in front of the body side by side. Move both hands toward the center changing to the handshape W.*

*See The Handshapes, p. 4 – 7.

Sign Synonym: microwave oven

 The hand creates the shape of **Wavy O** beginning with the handshape Oval O. Then move only the thumb so that it touches the tip of the fourth finger.

Visualize the word **FEW** as feeling something tiny on the fingertips.

The first hand takes the shape of Wavy O with the palm facing up. Slide the thumb across the fingertips ending on the outside of first finger.

Sign Synonym: several

Wavy O

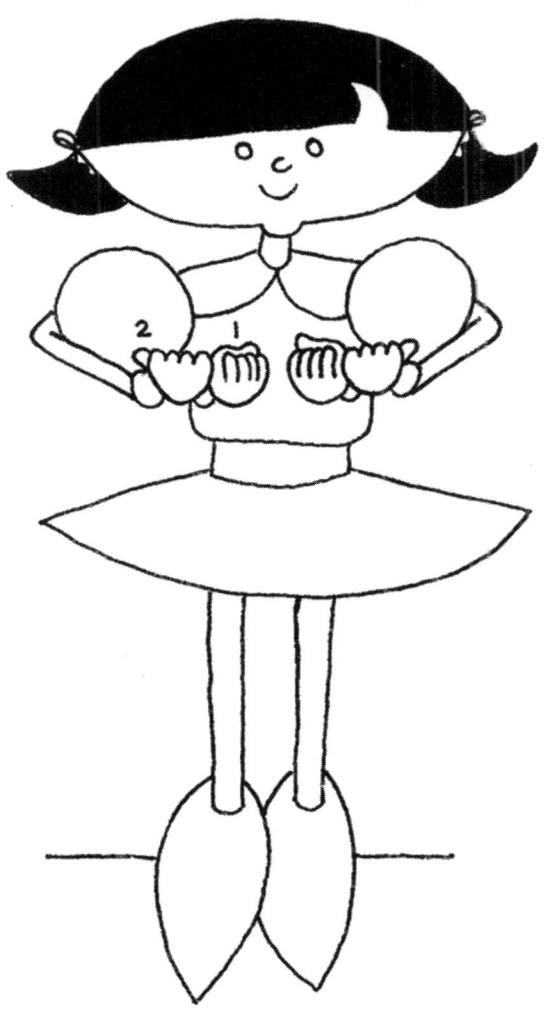

Using the Wavy O handshape also signs the word **PROPERTY** as if feeling the quality of the soil. Both hands take the shape of Wavy O with the palms facing up. Place both hands in front of the body side by side. Slide the thumbs back and forth on the fingertips a few times.

Sign Synonyms: dirt, ground, land, material, soil

 The hand creates the shape of **P** as the first finger points up and the second finger points up diagonally with the thumb resting on the lower joint of the second finger. The last two fingers fold down to the palm. Then bend the hand down at the wrist.

Visualize the word **PEOPLE** by seeing a large crowd excited for the concert to begin. Both hands take the shape of P with the palms facing down. Place the hands side by side. Alternate both hands in a forward circular motion.

Sign Synonyms: folk, population

P

Using the P handshape also signs the word **POLITICS** showing ideas about the government.

The first hand takes the shape of P with the palm facing the front. Place the hand near the side of the forehead. Twist the hand so that the palm faces the head; touch the second finger on the side of the forehead.

Sign Synonyms: Pierre (South Dakota), political, politician

The hand creates the shape of **Q** as the first finger is parallel with the thumb and the last three fingers fold down to the palm. Then bend the hand down at the wrist.

Visualize the word **QUEEN** by her royal sash that covers the shoulder and ends at the waist. The hand takes the shape of Q with the palm facing down. Lay the first finger and the thumb on the upper chest at the opposite side of the body. Shift the hand in diagonal motion from the upper chest to the other side of the body at the waist.

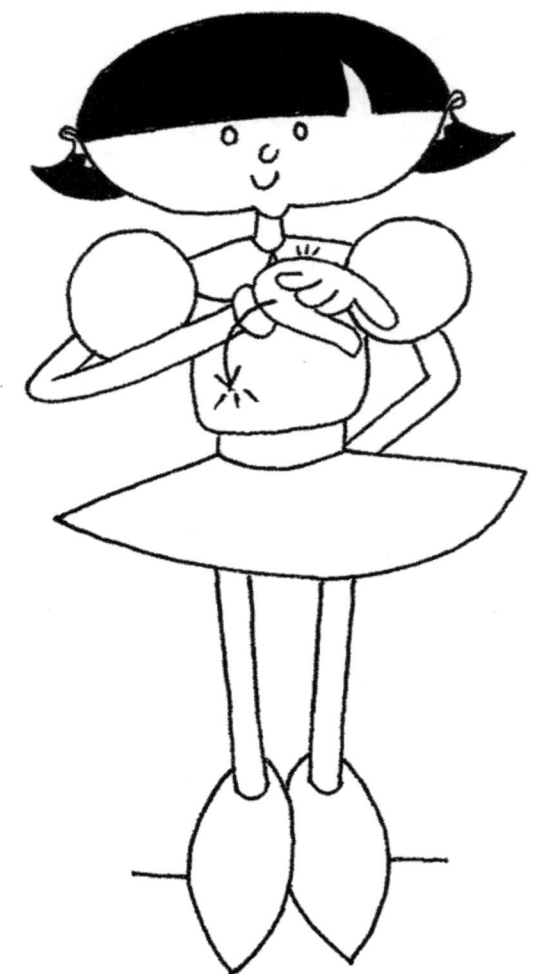

Q

Using the Q handshape also signs the word **QUALITY** to symbolize a person's above average characteristics.

The first hand takes the shape of Q with the palm facing down. Place the hand near the upper chest of the opposite side of the body. Shift the hand in a circular motion and then land the hand on the front of that shoulder.

Sign Synonyms: qualification, qualify

The hand creates the shape of **R** as the first finger points up and the second finger crosses it to rest on the back of the first finger. The last two fingers fold down to the palm, and the thumb rests across the third finger. The **R** handshape is just like crossing the first two fingers as if saying, "I hope so!"

Visualize the word **ROCKET** to symbolize a rocket moving straight up from a launch pad. The first hand takes the shape of R with the palm facing the front. The second hand takes the shape of B-L with the palm facing the side. Place the first hand on the palm of the second hand. Slide the first hand upward and above the second hand into the air, as in a lift-off.

Sign Synonym & Phrase: skyrocket, space rocket

R

Using the R handshape also signs the word **RESEARCH**. Visualize flipping through many pages to find specific information. The first hand takes the shape of R with the palm facing down. The second hand takes the shape of B-L with the palm facing up. Place the first hand's first two fingers at the center of the palm of the second hand. Slide the two fingers forward and across the palm of the second hand. Continue moving the first hand into the air in a circular motion, landing back at the original position. Repeat the motion a few times.

 The hand creates the shape of **R-L** as the first finger points up and the second finger crosses it to rest on the back of the first finger while the thumb points out and apart. The last two fingers fold down to the palm.

Visualize the word **REVIEW** as looking back through files.

The first hand takes the shape of R-L with the palm facing down; the second hand takes the shape of B-L with the palm facing the side. Place the tip of the first hand's thumb on the palm of the second hand. Rotate the first hand back while the thumb is still touching the palm of the second hand, ending with the first hand's palm facing the front.

R-L

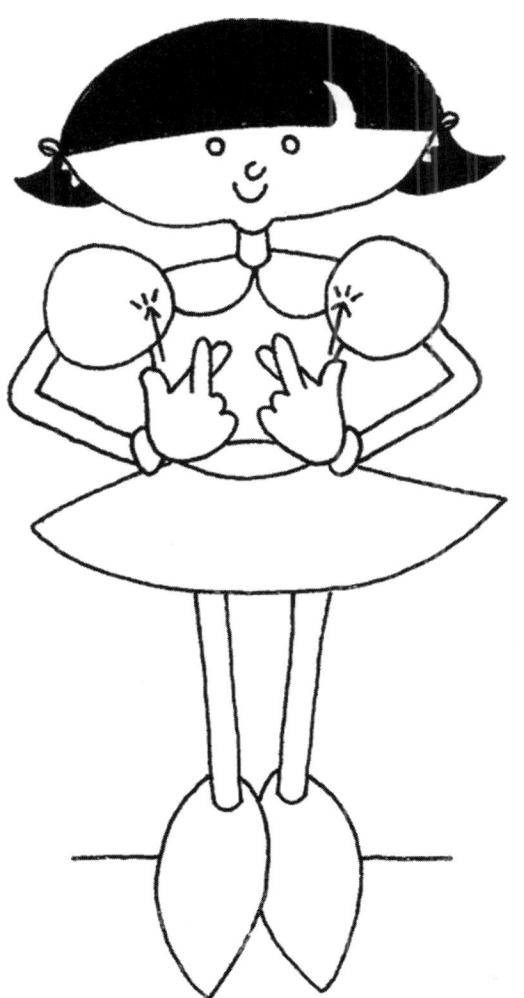

Using the R-L handshape also signs the word **RETIREMENT**.

Both hands take the shape of R-L with the palms facing down. Turn both hands at the wrist to touch the thumbs of both hands to each side of the chest.

Sign Synonym: retire

 The hand creates the shape of **S** as the four fingers curve down to close at the palm and the thumb rests across the closed fingers. The **S** handshape looks like a fist.

Visualize the word **YES** by nodding a head. The first hand takes the shape of S with the palm facing the front. Move the wrist in an arching up and down.

Sign Synonyms and Phrase: uh-huh, yeah, yup

S

Using the S handshape also signs the word **SENATOR** as a closed meeting of the members of Congress.

The hand takes the shape of S placing the side of the hand on the opposite upper chest with the palm facing the side. Shift the hand in a sideways arching motion landing on the other side of the upper chest. Did our **SENATOR** vote **YES**?

Sign Synonym: senate

 The hand creates the shape of **T** as all four fingers fold down to the palm; then the thumb is inserted between the first and second finger.

Visualize the word **TEAM** as gathering together in a circle.

Both hands take the shape of T with the palms facing the front. Touch the first fingers side by side. Move the hands in a semi-circular motion while twisting the wrists. Touch the last fingers together with the palms facing the body.

T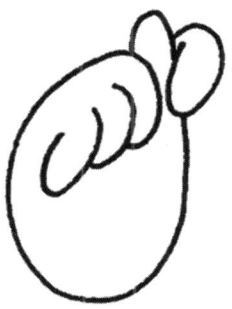

Using the T handshape also signs the word **TUESDAY**, the third day of the week.

The first hand takes the shape of T with the palm facing the body. Move the whole forearm in a small circle.

 The hand creates the shape of **U** as the first two fingers points up together while the last two fingers fold down to the palm. The thumb rests on the third finger.

Visualize the word **TRAIN** as connected to the road signs at a railroad track crossing. Both hands take the shape of U with the palms facing down. Place the first two fingers on top of the second hand's first two fingers at a perpendicular angle. The two hands will form an "X" shape. Then slide the first hand across the second hand's fingers a few times in a back and forth motion.

Sign Synonym & Phrases: go by train, railroad, travel by train

U

Using the U handshape also signs the word **WEIGHT** as balancing a heavy object on the scale.

Both hands take the shape of U. Crisscrossing the hands, place the second finger of the first hand on top of the first finger of the second hand. Move the first hand like a seesaw a few times.

Sign Synonyms: pound, scale, weigh

 The hand creates the shape of **V** as the first two fingers point up and apart while the last two fingers fold down to the palm; the thumb rests on the third finger.

Visualize the words **POINT OF VIEW** as looking at an item from different sides. The first hand takes the shape of 2 palm facing down; and the second hand takes the shape of 1 with palm facing forward. Move the first hand in a semi-circular motion pointing the first two fingers at the first finger of the second hand throughout the movement.

Sign Synonyms and Phrase: perspective, standpoint, view point

V

Using the V handshape also signs the word **DANCE** as moving the body in a rhythmic pattern. The first hand takes the shape of V. Then bend the first hand at the wrist so the first two fingers are pointing down. The second hand takes the shape of B-L with the palm facing up. Place the first hand above the palm of the second hand. Swing the first hand at the wrist, in an arching motion, back and forth a few times touching the second hand's palm halfway through the swing motion. Repeat the motion a few times.

Sign Synonyms: ballet, disco, gala, waltz

 The hand creates the shape of **Bent V** as the first two fingers point up and then bend at the tips; the last two fingers fold down to the palm with the thumb resting on the third finger.

Visualize the word **BONE** as if two bones are crisscrossing each other.

Both hands take the shape of Bent V with the palms facing the body. Place the first wrist behind the second wrist in front of the body.

Bent V

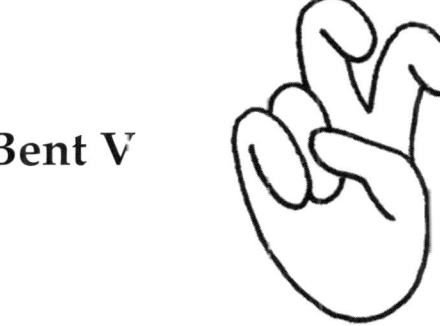

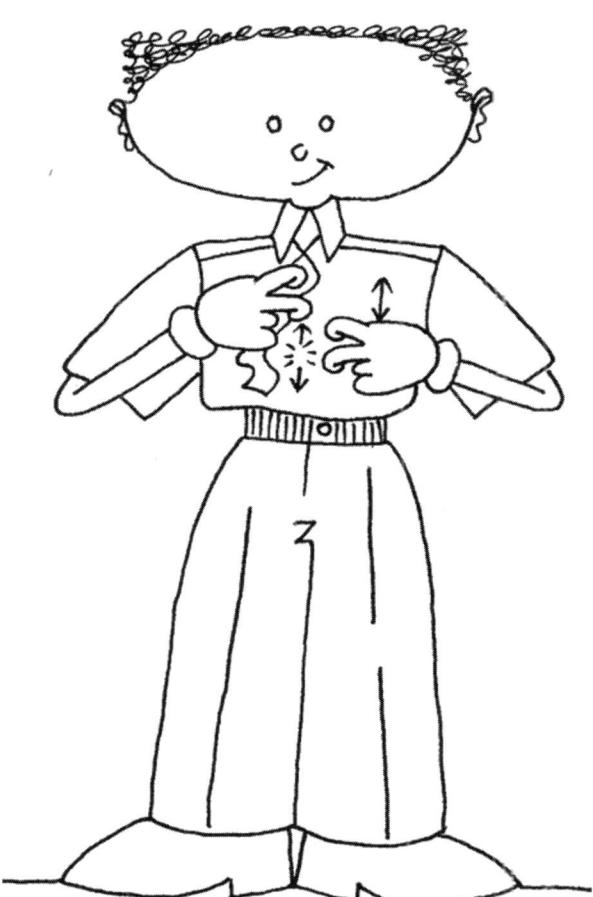

Using the Bent V handshape also signs the word **PROBLEM** as working through a process. Both hands take the shape of Bent V with the palms facing the body. Then rotate both hands at the wrists so that the knuckles end facing each other. Place the first hand higher than the second hand. Alternate the first two fingers of both hands in an up and down motion, striking the knuckles as the hands pass each other.

Sign Synonym: difficult

 The hand creates the shape of **W** as the first three fingers point up and apart while the last finger touches the thumb.

Sign the word **WATER** visualizing the W going toward the mouth as if drinking some **WATER**.

The hand takes the shape of W with the palm facing the side. Tap the first finger on the chin a few times.

W

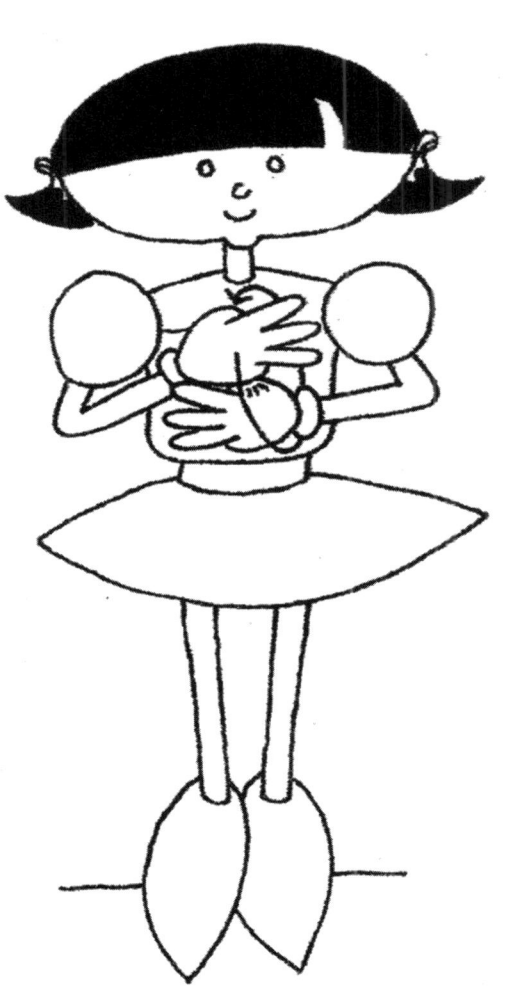

Using the W handshape also signs the word **WORLD** showing the rotation of the earth. Both hands take the shape of W placing the first hand on top of the second hand with the palms facing each other. Rotate the first hand forward and down in a circle around the second hand. Both hands end up back in the original position.

 The hand creates the shape of **X** as the first finger bends down to the second knuckle while the last three fingers fold down to the palm. The thumb rests across the second and third finger. The first finger will look like a hook.

Visualize the word **DONATE** as giving things or money away to help others.

Both hands take the shape of X with the palms facing each other. Shift both hands forward in an arching motion.

Sign Synonyms: charity, contribution, donation, gift, giving, grant, tribute

X

Using the X handshape also signs the word **NEED** as though tapping on a table. The first hand takes the shape of X placed in front of the body with the palm facing the front. Move the hand in an arching motion, up and down at the wrist, a few times.

Sign Synonyms & Phrase: necessary, should, supposed to

 The hand creates the shape of **X-A** as the first finger bends down in the X shape while the last three fingers fold down. The thumb rests on top of the first finger's X shape.

Visualize the word **DRUM** as using the sticks to make noise.

Both hands take the shape of X-A with the palms facing to each other in front of the body. Alternate both hands in a straight motion up and down. Repeat the motion.

Sign Synonym: xylophone

X-A

Using the X-A handshape also signs the word **CELEBRATION** as if twisting noisy party favors.

Both hands take the shape of X-A with the palms facing each other. Place the hands above the shoulders. Move both hands outward in a small circular motion a few times and smile.

Sign Synonyms: anniversary, celebrate, ceremony, festival

The hand creates the shape of **X-L** as the first finger bends down in the X shape while the last three fingers fold down to the palm. The thumb then points out to the side.

Visualize the word **WHO** as if asking, "Who is speaking?"

The first hand takes the shape of X-L with the thumb placed on the chin, palm facing the side. Wiggle the first finger a few times with the facial expression of the lips in an O-shape.

Sign Synonyms: whom, whose

X-L

Using the X-L handshape also signs the word **SUBSCRIBE** as signing up to receive a magazine in the mail.

The first hand creates the shape of X-L in front of the body near the shoulder with the palm facing the body. Move the hand downward while changing the shape to X-A.

Sign Synonyms: allowance, pension, royalty, subscription, welfare

 The hand creates the shape of **X-O** as the first finger bends down in the X shape while the last three fingers fold down to the palm. The thumb touches the tip of the first finger.

Visualize the word **EXACT** as pinpointing the exact place of an object. Both hands take the shape of X-O with the palms of both hands facing to each other and the first hand a little bit higher than the second hand. Move the first hand in a downward spiral movement landing on the first finger and thumb of the second hand.

Sign Synonyms: accuracy, accurate, concise, exactly, precise

X-O

Using the X-O handshape also signs the word **REVENGE** as though someone is striking back. Both hands take the shape of X-O with the first hand below the second hand. The palm of the first hand faces up while the palm of the second hand faces down. Shift the first hand up stopping when the first hand touches the first finger and the thumb of the second hand.

Sign Synonyms & Phrases: avenge, fight back, get even, retaliate, vengeance

The hand creates the shape of **X-T** as the first finger bends down in the X shape while the last three fingers fold down to the palm. Then place the thumb between the first and second fingers with the thumbnail touching the first finger.

Visualize the word **REMOVE** as a motion of flicking a bug away from someone else's shoulder.

The first hand takes the shape of X-T with the palm facing the body. Move the hand sideways while changing the handshape to X-L.

Sign Synonyms: abolish, abort, delete, eliminate, omit, reject, repel, rid, terminate

X-T

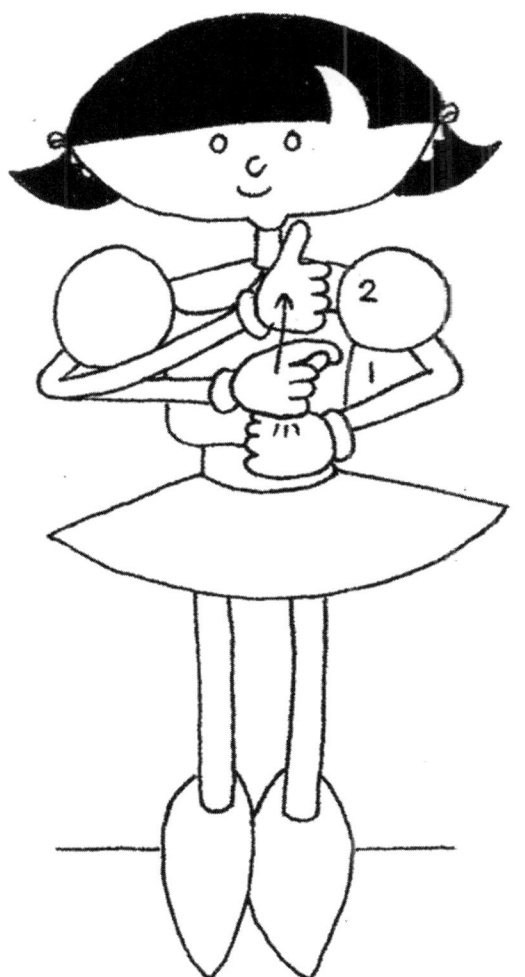

Using the X-T handshape also signs the word **CHAMPAGNE** as holding a bottle and popping out the cork.

The first hand takes the shape of X-T and the second hand takes the shape of S. Place the first hand on top of the second hand to represent the bottle and its cork. Raise the first hand up a little while changing the handshape to 10.*

*See The Handshapes, p. 4 – 7.

The hand creates the shape of **Y** as the first three fingers fold down to the palm. The thumb and fourth finger point out to the sides.

Visualize the word **PLAY** as rattling a toy. Both hands take the shape of Y with the palms facing each other shoulder-width apart. Rotate both hands at the wrist in a back and forth motion a few times.

Sign Synonyms: party, romp

Y

Using the Y handshape also signs the word **TODAY** as now or in this moment.

Both hands take the shape of Y with the palms facing up. Move both hands in a small up and down motion a few times.

Sign Synonyms: current, modern, present, urgent

The hand creates the shape of **Z** as the first finger points while the last three fingers fold down to the palm and the thumb rests across the second finger. The first finger makes an "imaginary line" as if drawing the letter Z in the air.

Visualize the word **LIGHTNING** as a bolt of lightning from the sky striking the ground. Both hands take the shape of Z, placed high in front of the chest, and the tips of the first fingers touch. Move the first hand down in a zigzag motion.

Z

Using the Z handshape also signs the word **VARIETY** as having an assortment of many things.

Both hands take the shape of Z with the tips of the first fingers touching and with both palms facing down. Alternate both hands up and down in a zigzag pattern while moving the hands away from each other.

Sign Synonyms: assortment, diversity, various

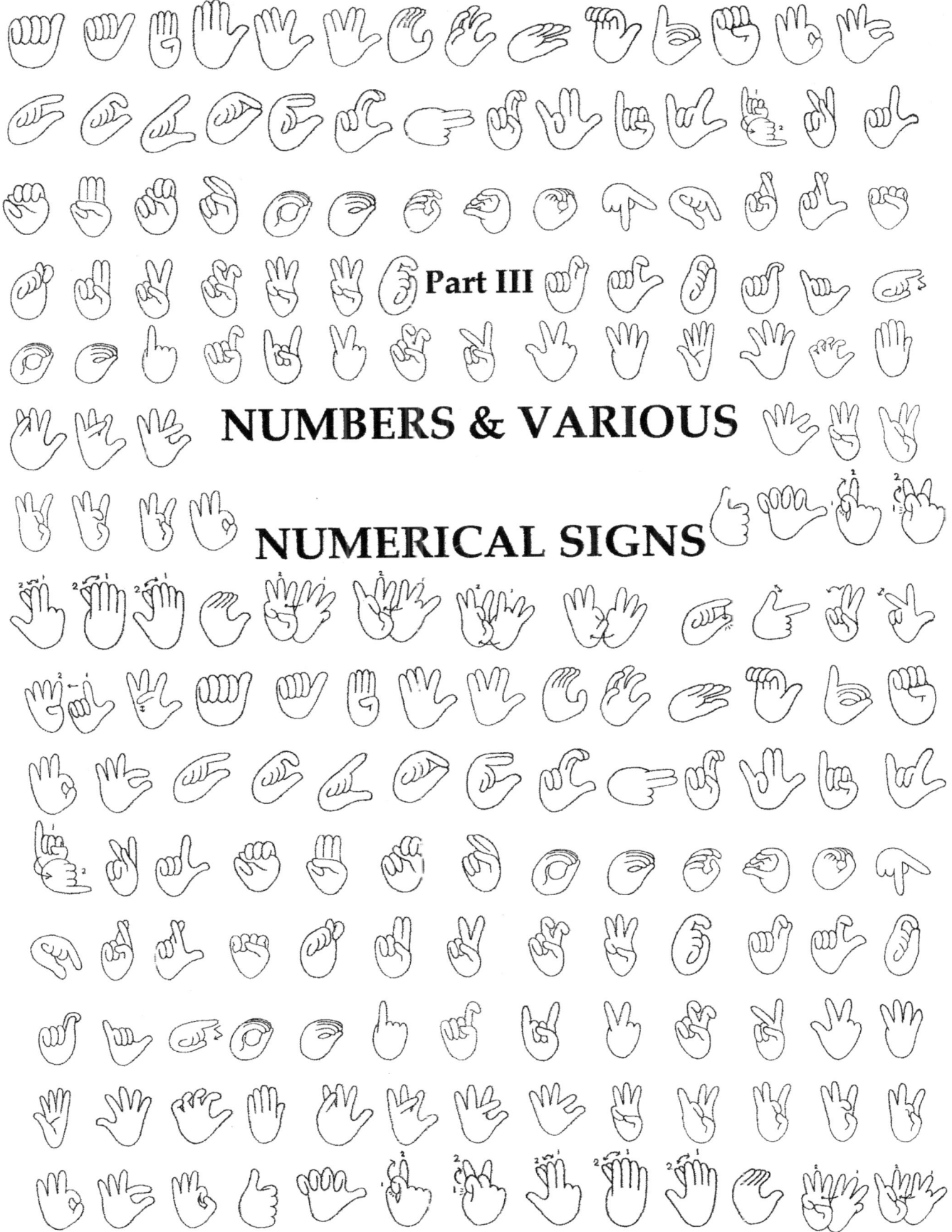

Part III

NUMBERS & VARIOUS NUMERICAL SIGNS

GUIDE TO RHYMING THE NUMBERS AND NUMERICAL SIGNS

Rhyming numbers in sign language is a simple technique to remember the numerical signs. This book gives examples for the numbers zero through twenty-five. Visualizing the words "kid" and "camp" or "girl" and "sport," you will see the words rhyme because they use the same handshapes. Signing the words "seven days" and "seven nights" or "eighteen million" and "eighteen inches," you see the same number handshape can show a variety of times and measurements.

It is very important to follow the positions for the numerical signs, specifically noticing which direction the palm faces for each number. The numbers from one through five, eleven through fifteen and twenty-one show the palm facing the body. The numbers from six through nine, sixteen through nineteen, twenty, and twenty-three through twenty-five show the palm facing out, away from the body. The numbers zero and ten show the palm facing the side. The number twenty-two shows the palm facing down.

In addition, for most of the numerical signs, there are two parts. As you read, you will see that the first part is the handshape. Part two is often the movement which completes the sign. This is especially true for the numbers ten through twenty-five. This movement can be a back and forth motion, a twisting motion, a sideways motion, or changing from one handshape to a different handshape.

The hand creates the shape of **Zero** as the first four fingers curve down together to touch the thumb as it curves up.

Visualize the phrase **NONE** as there is nothing there.

Both hands take the shape of Zero with the palms facing each other. Rattle both hands in an in-and-out motion: both hands in and then both hands out. Repeat a few times.

Sign Synonyms & Phrases: I have no, none of that, nobody, nothing, there is nothing (for)

Zero

Using the Zero handshape also signs the word **OPINION** as if beginning to understand someone's beliefs.

The first hand takes the shape of Zero with the palm facing the side. Place the hand near the forehead. Rattle the hand up and down a few times.

 The hand creates the shape of **Oval Zero** as the first four fingers bend down together to point straight to the side. All four fingers curve a little bit to allow the curved thumb to touch the tips of the fingers.

Visualize the word **EXPENSIVE** as taking money and wasting it away. The first hand takes the shape of Oval Zero with the palm facing down. The second hand takes the shape of B-L with the palm facing the body. Place the first hand's fingertips on the palm of the second hand. Move the first hand up and then out to the side while changing the shape to 5.*

*See The Handshapes, p. 4 – 7.

Sign Synonym: costly

Oval Zero

Using the Oval Zero handshape also signs the word **FOOD** as picking up something small to eat.

The first hand takes the shape of Oval Zero with the palm facing the mouth. Tap the fingertips and the thumb on the lips a few times.

Sign Synonyms: dine, eat

 The hand creates the shape of **1** as the first finger points up while the last three fingers fold down to the palm with the thumb resting across the second and third fingers. The palm faces the body.

Visualize the word **THINK** by pointing to the forehead.

The first hand takes the shape of 1 with the palm facing the head. Place the tip of the first finger on the forehead. What are you **THINKING** right now?

Sign Synonyms: mental, mind, thought

1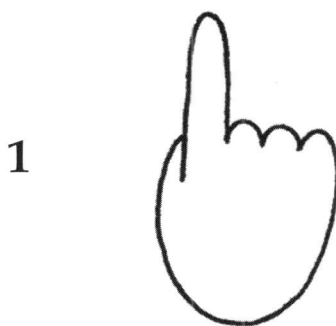

Using the 1 handshape also signs the word **POSITIVE** by using the addition symbol. Both hands take the shape of 1. Crisscrossing the hands, place the first finger of the first hand behind the first finger of the second hand making a plus sign with these two fingers. Tap the first finger of the first hand on the first finger of the second hand a few times.

Sign Synonym & Phrase: optimism, many pluses

 The hand creates the shape of **Bent 1** as the first finger bends while the last three fingers fold down to the palm as the thumb rests across the second and third fingers.

Visualize the word **ELECTRICITY** as bringing two wires together. Both hands take the shape of Bent 1. Place both hands side by side with the palms facing the body. Move both hands back and forth in sideways motion tapping the first fingers together a few times.

Sign Synonyms: battery, electric, power

Bent 1

Using the Bent 1 handshape also signs the word **COST** as if someone is putting the price tag on an item.

The first hand takes the shape of Bent 1 with the palm facing the side and the second hand takes the shape of B-L with the palm facing the body. Place the first hand above the second hand. Slide the first hand past the second hand touching the palm of the second hand on the way down.

Sign Synonyms: charge, fare, fee, fine, price, tax, toll

 The hand creates the shape of **1-I** as the first and fourth fingers point up while the second and third finger fold down to the palm. The thumb rests across the second and third fingers.

Visualize the word **KID** as the one with the runny nose.

The first hand takes the shape of 1-I with the palm facing down. Touch the first finger of the first hand to the face just below the nose. Wiggle the hand up and down, leaving the first finger in place.

Sign Synonym: kids

1-I

Using the 1-I handshape also signs the word **CAMP** as if seeing a tent set up in the trees. Both hands take the shape of 1-I with the palms facing each other. The first finger of the first hand touches the first finger of the second hand. In the same way, the fourth fingers touch each other. Pull the hands apart in a short, downward diagonal motion. How many **KIDS** were at your **CAMP**?

Sign Synonyms: camping, tent

The hand creates the shape of **2** as the first two fingers point up and apart while the last two fingers fold down to the palm with the thumb resting across the third finger. The palm faces the body.

Visualize the word **SEE** as showing what is in your field of vision.
The first hand takes the shape of 2 with the palm facing to the body. Place the first hand on your upper cheek with your middle finger touching your face just below one eye. Move the first hand forward a short distance. Do you **SEE** all of your **OPPORTUNITIES**?

Sign Synonyms: sight, visualize

2

Using the 2 handshape also signs the word **VOICE**.

The first hand takes the shape of 2 placing the tips of the fingers at the base of the neck. The palm naturally faces the body. Move the hand up and forward in an arching motion, following the arch of the neck. Stop a short distance in front of the chin.

Sign Synonyms: vocal, volume

 The hand creates the shape of **Bent 2** as the first two fingers point up and apart while the last two fingers fold down to the palm with the thumb resting across the third finger. Then bend the first two fingers forward.

Visualize the word **TOUR** as going on a trip from one place to another. The first hand takes the shape of Bent 2 with the palm facing the front. Move the hand down an arching motion to the side.

Sign Synonyms: journey, travel, transfer, trip

Bent 2

Using the Bent 2 handshape also signs the word **TICKET** as if punching hole to validate the ticket.

The first hand takes the shape of Bent 2 with the palm facing down. The second hand takes the shape of B-L with the palm facing the body. Move both hands toward each other and insert the second hand between the first and second finger on the first hand.

 The hand creates the shape of **2-K** as the first finger points up and the second finger points forward diagonally. The last two fingers fold down to the palm and the thumb rests on the third finger.

Visualize the word **DOUBLE** as getting twice as much as the normal amount.

The first hand takes the shape of 2-K. The second hand takes the shape of B-L with the palm facing the side. Place the second finger of the first hand on the palm of the second hand. Slide the first hand up and away from the palm of the second hand moving in a semi-circular motion so the palm of the first hand ends with facing up.

Sign Synonym: twice

2-K

Using the 2-K handshape also signs the word **BORROW** as getting something from someone. Both hands take the shape of 2-K with the first two fingers of each hand pointing forward and both palms facing each other. Place the first hand on top of the second hand. Shift both hands in an arching motion toward the body.

Sign Synonym Phrase: lend me

The hand creates the shape of **3** as the first and second finger point up and apart and the thumb points out while the last two fingers fold down to the palm. The palm faces the body.

Visualize the word **PARK** as the car resting in the parking spot.

The first hand takes the shape of 3 with the palm facing the side and the second hand takes the shape of B-L with the palm facing up. Place the first hand above the second hand. Move the first hand down to **PARK** on the palm of the second hand.

3

Using the 3 handshape also signs the word **GARAGE** as parking under a roof.

The first hand takes the shape of 3 with the palm facing the body and the second hand takes the shape of B-L with the palm facing down. Place the first hand underneath the second hand. Move the first hand in and out from under the second hand a few times.

The hand creates the shape of **Bent 3** as the first and second fingers and the thumb point up and apart and then bend down. The last two fingers fold down to the palm.

Visualize the word **PITCH** as throwing a baseball.

The first hand takes the shape of Bent 3. Place the hand above the shoulder with the palm facing the front. Move the hand forward in a quick short thrust.

Sign Synonym: pitcher

Bent 3

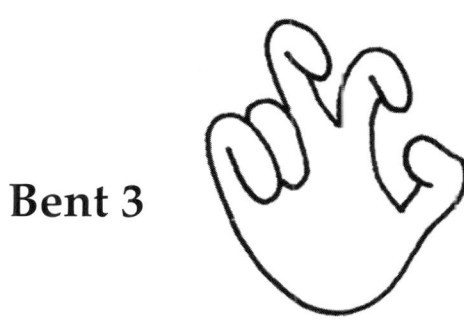

Using the Bent 3 handshape also signs the word **CHAMPION** as if someone is putting a crown on your head. The first hand takes the shape of Bent 3 with the palm facing down and the second hand takes the shape of 1 with the palm facing the side. Place the first hand above the second hand. Move the first hand down until the palm touches the first finger of the second hand.

Sign Synonym: championship

 The hand creates the shape of **3-K** as the first finger and the thumb point up and out and the second finger points forward diagonally while the last two fingers fold down to the palm.

Visualize the word **TRIPLE** as an ice cream cone with three different flavors, a **TRIPLE** dip cone. The first hand takes the shape of 3-K. The second hand takes the shape of B-L with the palm facing the side. Place the second finger of the first hand on the palm of the second hand. Slide the first hand up and away from the palm of the second hand moving in a semi-circular so the first hand ends with the palm facing up.

3-K

Using the 3-K handshape also signs the word THIRD as if taking THIRD place in a race.

The first hand takes the shape of 3-K with the palm facing the body. Move the hand out to the side.

 The hand creates the shape of **4** as all four fingers point up and apart while the thumb folds down to the palm. The palm faces the body.

Visualize the word **JAIL** as seeing the criss-crossing bars.

Both hands take the shape of 4 with the palms facing the body. Turn the first hand at the wrist so the fingers point to the side. Place the first hand's fingers behind the second hand's fingers. Tap the first hand on the second hand once.

Sign Synonyms: cage (as in bird cage), prison

4

Using the 4 handshape also signs the word **FENCE** as seeing the horizontal planks on a wooden fence.

Both hands take the shape of 4 with the palms facing the body. Bring both hands together to touch at the fingertips. Separate the hands by moving each hand apart to its respective side.

Sign Synonym Phrase: privacy fence

 The hand creates the shape of **Open 4** as all four fingers point up and apart while the thumb points away from the palm.

Visualize the word **LEARN** as if copying information from a book and absorbing it into your mind.

The first hand takes the shape of Open 4 with the palm facing down and the second hand takes the shape of B-L with the palm facing up. Place the tips of the first hand's fingers and thumb on the palm of the second hand. Lift the first hand off the second hand while changing the handshape to Oval Zero. End the sign by placing the fingertips of the first hand on the forehead. What did you **LEARN** today?

Sign Synonyms: learned, learning

Open 4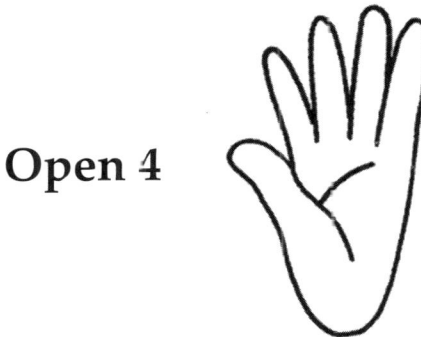

Using the Open 4 handshape also signs the word **EXPERIENCE** as if remembering something that you learned before.

The first hand takes the shape of Open 4. Place the first hand at the side of the face with the fingers and thumb touching the cheek. Slide all four fingers down the cheek and move the hand away from the head as you change to the handshape of Oval Zero.

Sign Synonym: ordeal

The hand creates the shape of **5** as all the fingers and the thumb point out and apart. The palm faces the body.

Visualize the word **AMERICA** as the fingers representing the people from many countries coming together to live in United States. Both hands take the shape of 5 with the palms facing each other. Interlock the fingers of both hands together. Move the hands around in a small circle in front of the body.

Sign Synonym: American

5

Using the 5 handshape also signs the word **TREES** as seeing many branches fluttering in the wind.

The first hand takes the shape of 5 with the palm facing the side and the second hand takes the shape of BL with the palm facing down and the fingers pointing to the side. Touch the elbow of the first hand on the second hand. Rotate the first hand at the wrist back and forth a few times.

Sign Synonyms: forest(s), tree, woods

 The hand creates the shape of **Bent 5** as all the fingers and the thumb point out and apart. Then bend all the fingers forward leaving the thumb as it was.

Visualize the word **TIGER** as noticing his long whiskers.

Both hands take the shape of Bent 5 with the palms facing the body and the thumbs pointing up. Place all the fingertips on the cheeks. Brush each cheek as you slide both hands across the cheeks and away from the face.

Bent 5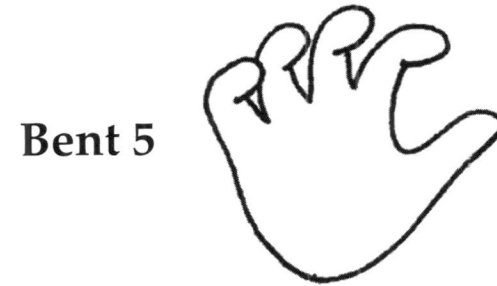

Using the Bent 5 handshape also signs the word **ROAR** as shouting with a long, deep sound. The first hand takes the shape of Bent 5 with the palm facing the head. Place the fingertips just in front of the mouth. Move the hand up in an arching motion forward and away from the face.

Sign Synonyms & Phrase: growl, scream, shout, to cry out, yell

 The hand creates the shape of **Closed 5** as all the fingers and thumb point up together side by side.

Visualize the word **MUSIC** as seeing a conductor directing an orchestra. Both hands take the shape of Closed 5. Position one arm as if it is reaching out. Keep the elbow close to the body and the palm facing up. The other hand is placed a little bit above the outstretched arm with the palm facing the body. Swing this hand in a downward arching motion along the forearm of the other hand. Repeat this motion in a back and forth movement a few times. Do you see your hand directing the **MUSIC**?

Sign Synonyms: anthem, band, choir, concert, harmony, hymn, melody, musical, sing, song

Closed 5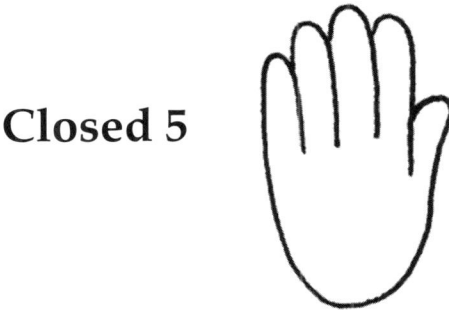

Using the Closed 5 handshape also signs the word **APPRECIATION** as if you've just finished a meal that someone made only for you.

Both hands take the shape of Closed 5 with the palms facing the body. Place the first hand on the chest and the second hand on the body just below the first hand. Keeping the hands touching the body, move both hands in a circular motion back to their original positions. Continue the circular movement for a few more circles.

Sign Synonyms: appreciate, enjoy, leisure, pleasure

 The hand creates the shape of **5-6** as all the fingers and thumb point out and apart. Then move the last finger forward.

Visualize the phrase **FIVE-FOLD** as meeting a happy farmer who has five times as much crops as compared to last year. The first hand takes the shape of 5-6 and the second hand takes the shape of 5 with both palms facing each other. Touch the last finger of the first hand on the palm of the second hand. In a semi-circular motion, slide the first hand up and away from the palm of the second hand. Stop the movement when the palm of the first hand is facing up.

5-6

Using the 5-6 handshape also signs the word **PREPARATORY** as in a year of schooling, after high school, that some students need to take before being accepted into college.

The first hand takes the shape of 5 with the palm facing the side and the forearm angled down. The second hand takes the shape of 5-6 with the palm facing the first hand. Tap the first hand's palm on the last finger of the second hand.

The hand creates the shape of **5-7** as all the fingers and the thumb point out and apart. Then move the ring finger forward.

Visualize the word **FRESHMAN** as the class of students in their first year of college. The first hand takes the shape of 5 with the palm facing the side and the forearm angled down. The second hand takes the shape of 5-7 with the palm facing the first hand. Tap the first hand's palm on the third finger of the second hand.

5-7

Using the 5-7 handshape also signs the words **RING FINGER** as putting on a wedding ring. With both palms facing each other, the first hand takes the shape of Open 9* and the second hand takes the shape of 5-7. Place the first hand's first finger and the thumb on the fingertip of the second hand's third finger. Slide the first hand all the way to the base of this third finger.

*See The Handshapes, p. 4 – 7.

Sign Synonym: ring

 The hand creates the shape of **5-8** as all the fingers and thumb point out and apart. Then move the middle finger forward.

Visualize the word **FEEL** as if sensing something in your heart.

The first hand takes the shape of 5-8 with the palm facing the body. Place the middle finger on the chest. Slide the hand up and forward in a small circular motion landing back at its original position. Repeat the motion.

Sign Synonyms & Phrase: feelings, I feel, sensation, sense

5-8

Using the 5-8 handshape also signs the word **LUCKY** as if giving a kiss for good luck.

The first hand takes the shape of 5-8 with the palm facing the head. Place the middle finger on the lip of the mouth. Move the hand in a semi-circular motion forward and away from the mouth ending with the palm facing the front. Are you feeling **LUCKY**?

Sign Synonyms: fortunate, luck

The hand creates the shape of **5-9** as all the fingers and the thumb point out and apart. Then move the first finger forward.

Visualize the word **NICKEL** as finding a five-cent coin laying head's up.

The first hand takes the shape of 5-9. Place the first finger on the forehead with the palm facing the head. Move the hand away from the head a short distance.

5-9

Using the 5-9 handshape also signs the word **JUNIOR** as the class of students in their third year of college.

The first hand takes the shape of 5 with the palm facing the side and the forearm angled down. The second hand takes the shape of 5-9 with the palm facing the first hand. Tap the first hand's palm on the first finger of the second hand.

The hand creates the shape of **6** as the first three fingers point up and apart while the last finger touches the thumb. For the number **6** the palm faces out, away from the body.

Visualize the words **SIX CANS** by signing the number 6 and a short glass. The first hand takes the shape of **6** with the palm facing the front. Then, sign **CANS** by changing the shape of the first hand to C with the palm facing the side. The second hand takes the shape of B-L with the palm facing up. Place the first hand on the palm of the second hand. Move the first hand straight up a short distance and back down to touch the palm again. Repeat this motion one more time.

Sign Synonyms for **CAN**: cup, glass

6

Using the 6 handshape also signs the words **SIX PACKAGES** by signing the number 6 and the box. The first hand takes the shape of **6** with the palm facing the front. Then, sign **PACKAGES** using in the shape of B-L. Start with both palms facing each other with about a foot of space in between them. Turn both hands at the wrists so both palms face the body keeping about the same space between the hands. Do you see the **PACKAGE** your hands just made?

Sign Synonyms & Phrases for **PACKAGE**: a case of, box, gift box, present, room

 The hand creates the shape of **7** as the first, second and the last finger point up and apart while the third finger bends down to touch the thumb.

Visualize the words **SEVEN DAYS** by signing the number seven and the sun rising and setting. The first hand takes the shape of **7** with the palm facing the front. Then, sign **DAYS** by changing the shape of the first hand to 1 with the palm facing the side. The second hand takes the shape of B-L. Place the second hand under and touching the elbow of the first hand with the palm facing down. The second hand's forearm is naturally horizontal across the body. Keeping the first hand's elbow touching the second hand, move the first hand in an arching motion ending with the forearm landing on the second hand's forearm.

Sign Synonyms & Phrase for **DAY**: all day, daytime, today

7

Using the 7 handshape also signs the words **SEVEN NIGHTS** by signing the number 7 and showing the sun setting under the horizon. The first hand takes the shape of **7** with the palm facing the front. Then, sign **NIGHTS** with both hands taking the shape of C-L with the palms facing down. Put the first hand a little bit above the second hand. Place the palm of the first hand on top of the second hand.

Sign Synonyms for **NIGHT**: dusk, evening, tonight

 The hand creates the shape of **8** as the first, third and last fingers point up and apart while the middle finger bends down to touch the thumb.

Visualize the words **EIGHT HUNDRED** by signing the number 8 and the Roman numeral for one hundred, C. The first hand takes the shape of **8** with the palm facing the front. Then, sign **HUNDRED** by changing the first hand to the C shape and moving a bit to the side.

8

Using the 8 handshape also signs the words **EIGHT DOLLARS** as if counting the number of people in a line.

The first hand takes the shape of 8 with the palm facing the front. Twist the hand at the wrist so that the palm faces the body. The movie ticket costs **EIGHT DOLLARS**.

Sign Synonym: eighth

 The hand creates the shape of **Open 8** as the middle finger bends forward to be parallel to the thumb while the other fingers are pointing up and apart.

Visualize the word **LIKE** as if you have chosen something you prefer over another thing.

The first hand takes the shape of Open 8 placing the middle finger and thumb on the chest. Move the hand forward changing the handshape to 8.

Open 8

Using the Open 8 handshape also signs the word **MESSAGE** as if you are reading a short note. Both hands take the shape of Open 8 with the fingers pointing up. Place both hands close together with the palms facing each other. Turn the second hand at the wrist so that hand's fingers point away from the body. Bring the hands close together while you change both hands to the handshape of 8. As your hands close to the handshape of 8 they will be touching one another. Then move your hands apart to the sides; both hands are now in the handshape of 8. Repeat this motion one more time. Did you receive my **MESSAGE**?

Sign Synonym: note

 The hand creates the shape of **8-S** as the middle finger curves inward and the thumb covers its fingernail while the other fingers point up and apart.

Visualize the word **LIGHT** as if someone is shining a flashlight in your face. The first hand takes the shape of 8-S with the palm facing the body. Place the thumb on the lips. Move the hand a little bit backward, away from the face, while changing the handshape to Open 8.

8-S

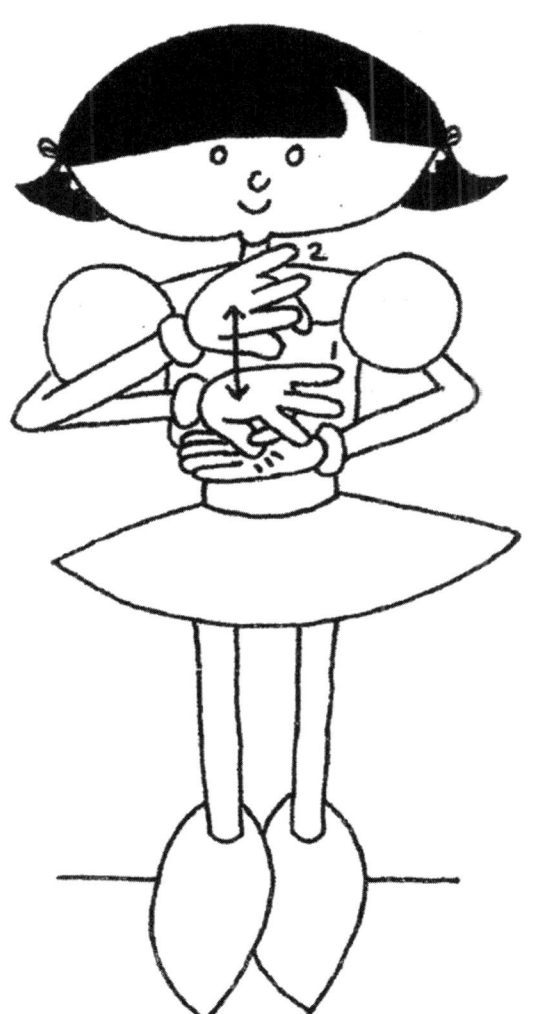

Using the 8-S handshape also signs the word **PUMPKIN** as though someone is thumping a melon to check for ripeness.

With the palms facing down, the first hand takes the shape of 8-S and the second hand takes the shape of B-L. Place the first hand above the second hand. Flick the middle finger of the first hand on the back of the second hand changing the handshape to Open 8. Repeat this motion a few times.

Sign Synonym: melon

 The hand creates the shape of **9** as the first finger curves down to meet the thumb and the last three fingers point up and apart.

Visualize the word **DESCRIBE** as pausing for a few moments to clarify your meanings. Both hands take the shape of 9 with the palms facing each other and the fingers pointing away from the body. Shift the first hand forward while shifting the second hand backward. Alternate both hands in a back and forth motion a few times.

Sign Synonyms: define, definition, description, explain, explanation

9

Using the 9 handshape also signs the word **FAITH** by placing your trust in another person or thing. Both hands take the shape of 9. Position the first finger and thumb of the first hand on the forehead with the palm facing the side. Place the second hand in front of the body with the palm facing the opposite side. Move the first hand down in an arching motion ending with the first hand's thumb and first finger landing on top of the second hand's thumb and first finger. **FAITH** can be hard to **DESCRIBE**.

Sign Synonym: faithful

The hand creates the shape of **Open 9** as the first finger bends forward to be parallel while the last three fingers point up and apart.

Visualize the word **FIND** by seeing something small and reaching out to pick it up.

The first hand takes the shape of Open 9 with the palm facing down. Place this hand out in front of the body. Move the hand up and backward while changing the shape of the hand to 9.

Sign Synonym & Phrase: found, pick up

Open 9

Using the Open 9 handshape also signs the word CAT as miming the feline's long whiskers. Both hands take the shape of Open 9 with the palms facing each other. Place the first finger and the thumb of both hands their respective cheeks. Move both hands away from the face, straight sideways, while changing the shape of both hands to 9.

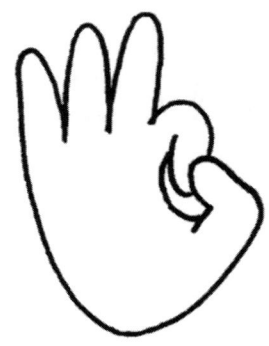

The hand creates the shape of **9-S** as the first finger curves inward and the thumb covers its fingernail while other fingers point up and apart.

Visualize the word **FOX** as showing the pointed snout of the animal.

The hand takes the shape of 9-S, placing the first finger and the thumb on the nose.

Rotate the hand back and forth around the nose by moving the wrist.

9-S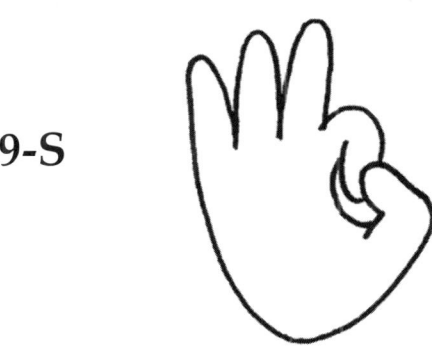

Using the 9-S handshape also signs the word **SPOT** as polka dots on a dress or a stain from lunch on your shirt.

The hand takes the shape of 9-S with the palm facing the side. Lay the first finger and the thumb with the other three fingers pointing up on the upper opposite chest.

Sign Synonym: stain

 The hand creates the shape of **10** as the thumb points up and the four fingers fold down to the palm. Then shake the hand a bit, as if trembling.

Visualize the word **GIRL** by tracing the ties of a young girl's bonnet from the early 1900s.

The first hand takes the shape of 10 with the palm facing the side of the head. Place the thumb on upper cheek and slide the hand down to the chin.

10

Using the 10 handshape also signs the word **SPORT** as facing each other in a race.

As both hands take the shape of 10, place the hands comfortably in front of the body with the palms facing each other. Twist both hands at the wrists in an alternating back and forth motion a few times.

Sign Synonyms: competition, contest, race

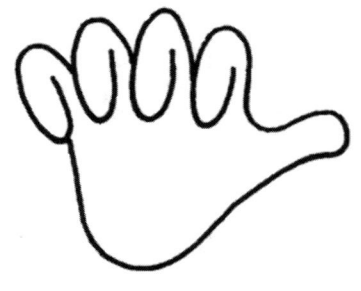 The hand creates the shape of **Wide 10** as all four fingers point up and apart. Fold all the fingers down to the palm keeping the fingers spaced apart. The thumb remains pointing straight out.

Visualize the word **MOTOR** by seeing engine parts in motion. Both hands take the shape of Wide 10 with the palms facing the body. Bend both wrists down so the knuckles face each other. Bring the two hands together so the knuckles loosely intersect. Move the hands up and down a few times. Is the **MOTOR** working right?

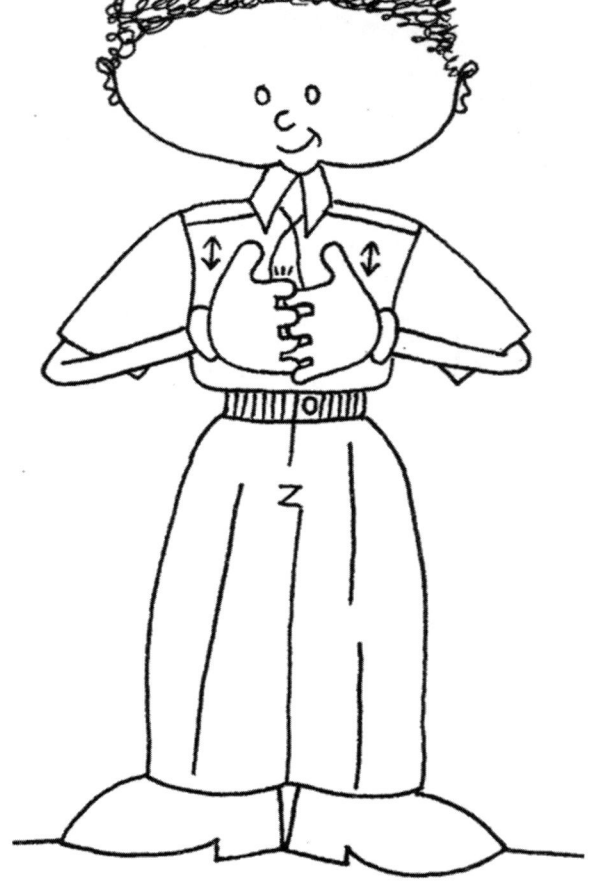

Sign Synonyms: engine, factory, industry, machine, manufacture

Wide 10

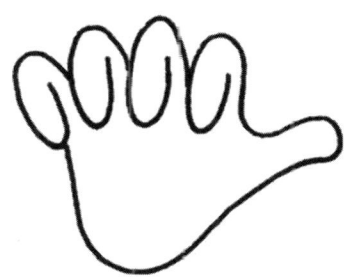

Using the Wide 10 handshape also signs the word **COMBINE** as to bring two things together. Both hands create the Wide 10 handshape with the palms facing the body. Bend both wrists down so the knuckles face each other. Then, move the hands together interlocking the knuckles.

Sign Synonyms & Phrase: combination, compatible, compatibility, consolidate, fit in, match, merge

The hand creates part one of the handshape for **11** as the first finger bends down and the thumb covers its fingernail. With the palm facing the body, the rest of the fingers fold down to the palm. Then, the motion for part two is to flick the first finger up and away from the thumb to stand up straight.

Visualize the word **ANNUAL** as something that pops up only once every year. The first hand takes the shape of 11 with the palm facing the body. The second hand takes the shape of S with the palm facing the side. Place the first hand on top of the second hand. Move the first hand up in a diagonal line while changing the handshape to the second part of 11. Immediately return the hand back to its original position. Repeat this motion twice.

Sign Synonym Phrase: every year

11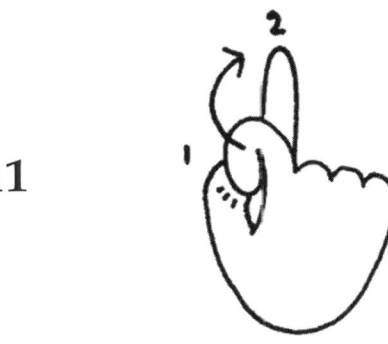

Using the 11 handshape also signs the word **POPCORN** as if seeing the kernels burst when making popcorn.

Both hands take the shape of 11 with the palms facing the body. Place both hands comfortably in front of the body. Move the first hand up changing the handshape to the second part of 11. At the same time, the second hand moves down returning to the first part of the handshape 11. Alternating hands, repeat this up and down a few times.

The hand creates part one of the handshape for **12** as the first two fingers bend down together and the thumb covers their fingernails. With the palm facing the body, the last two fingers fold down to the palm. Then, for part two, flick the first two fingers up and away from the thumb. These fingers point up and apart, similar to the handshape of 2.

Visualize the word **MIDNIGHT** as staying up late at night to see both hands of the clock point to twelve.

Put both arms in front of the body with the elbows bent so one forearm is on top of the other forearm. Angle the lower forearm down. The lower hand takes the shape of 12 with the palm facing the body. Then sign **MIDNIGHT** by changing to the second part of the handshape 12.

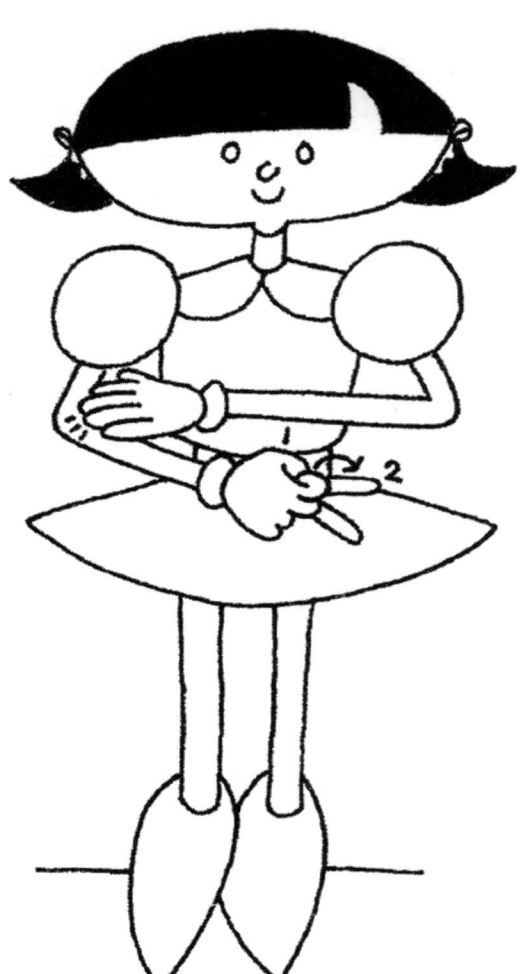

12

Using the 12 handshape also signs the word **FROG** as seeing the animal's throat getting bigger when it is croaking.

The first hand takes the shape of 12 with the palm facing down. Place the back of the hand under the chin. Flip the two fingers out to the second part of the handshape 12 and then back to the first position. Repeat the motion twice. Do you change into a **FROG** at **MIDNIGHT**?

Sign Synonym: toad

The hand creates part one of the handshape for **13** as the first and second finger point up together and the third and fourth finger fold down to the palm. With the palm facing the body, the thumb points out and apart. Then, for part two, move the first two fingers as if they are connected back and forth a few times.

Visualize the word **CUTE** as appreciating how sweet a kitten is by scratching his chin.

The first hand takes the shape of 13 with the palm facing the head. Place the fingertips on the chin. Slide the fingertips down towards the palm and away from the chin. Return the hand to its original position. Repeat the motion a few times.

13

Using the 13 handshape also signs the word **HORSE** by showing the ears of the animal. Both hands take the shape of 13 with the palms facing the front. Place the thumbs on each side of the forehead. Move the first two fingers of both hands back and forth a few times.

Sign Synonyms: bronco, colt, filly, mare, mustang, pony, stallion

 The hand creates part one of the handshape for **14** as all four fingers point up together. With the palm facing the body, fold the thumb in to lay across the palm. Then, for part two, move all four fingers back and forth a few times.

Visualize the word **TROUBLE** as the confusion that occurs when there is a car accident up ahead.

Both hands take the shape of 14 with the palms facing each other. Place the hands shoulder width apart near each side of the head. Move the forearms in until the hands cross each other right in front of the eyes. The first hand should be slightly behind the second hand so the hands do not hit each other. Move both hands back to their original positions. Repeat the motion but this time stop when the hands are crossed.

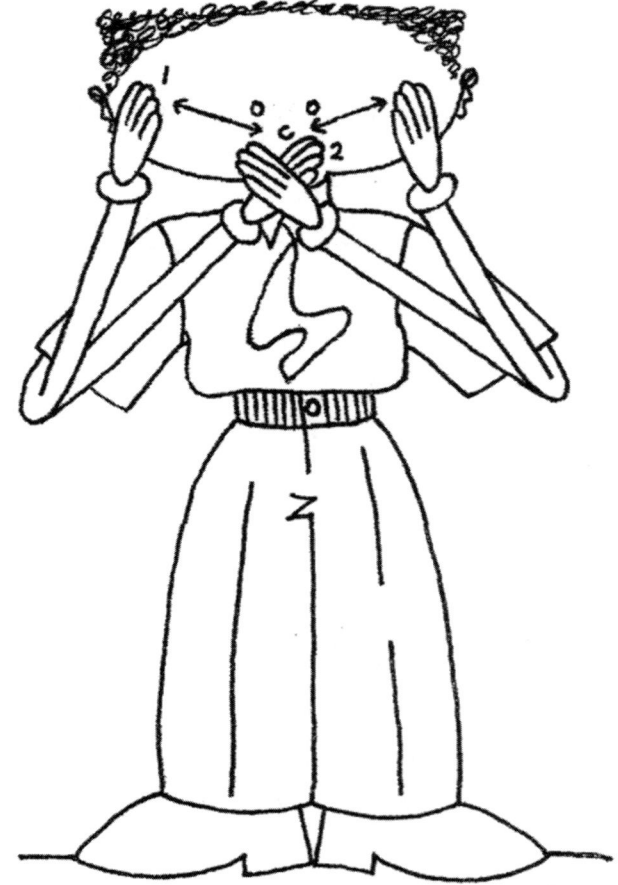

Sign Synonym: troublesome

14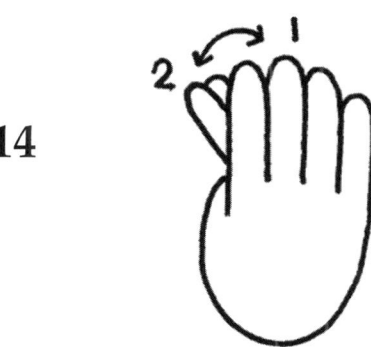

Using the 14 handshape also signs the word **DONKEY** by showing the long and wide ears of the animal.

Both hands take the shape of 14 with the palms facing front. Place the back of both hands on the each side of the forehead. Fold the fingers of both hands down and back up a few times. Did the **DONKEY** get you in **TROUBLE**?

Sign Synonym: mule

 The hand creates part one of the handshape for **15** as all the fingers points up together. With the palm facing the body, the thumb points out and apart. Then, for part two, move all four fingers back and forth a few times.

Visualize the word **BETTER** as if you are wiping the crumbs off to clean your face. The first hand takes the shape of 15 with the palm facing the head and the fingers pointing to the side. Place the fingertips on the lips. Slide the fingertips out and away from the face while changing to the handshape 10.

Sign Synonym: best

15

Using the 15 handshape also signs the word **BUTTERFLY** as seeing the beautiful insect flap its wings.

Both hands take the shape of 15 with both palms facing the body and the fingers pointing toward each other. Place the first hand in front of and touching the second hand. Slide the hands together until the thumbs touch; then bring the elbows down so the fingers are pointing up at an angle. Wave the fingers of both hands back and forth a few times. Do you see the **BUTTERFLY's** wings?

 The hand creates the shape of **Flat 15** as all the fingers point up together and then bend forward a bit. With the palm facing the body, the thumb points out and apart.

Visualize the word **YOUNG** as a youth's height is not higher than an adult's shoulders.

Both hands take the shape of Flat 15 with the palms facing the body. Place the fingertips on the upper chest. Slide both hands up to the shoulders and away from the body. Using a small circular movement, return both hands to their original positions. Repeat this motion two times.

Sign Synonyms: younger, youth

Flat 15

Using the Flat 15 handshape also signs the word **ADVANCE** as if rising to a higher level or stepping up on the ladder of success. Both hands take the shape of Flat 15 with the palms facing each other. Place the hands in front of the body above the shoulders. Pull both hands back a bit while raising the hands to a higher level.

Sign Synonyms: advanced, advancement, elevate, elevated, exalt, exalted, higher, highest, prominent, promote, promotion

The hand creates part one of the handshape for **16** as the first three fingers point up and apart and the last finger bends down to touch the thumb. Then, for part two, twist the hand at the wrist toward the side and to the front. End with the palm facing the front.

Visualize the words **SIXTEEN WEEKS** by signing the number 16 and show you the plans for the week on the calendar.

The first hand signs the number **16**. Then, sign **WEEKS** by changing the shape of the first hand to 1 with the palm facing the front. The second hand takes the shape of B-L with the palm facing the body and the fingers pointing to the side. Place the first hand on the palm of the second hand near its thumb. Slide the first hand across the palm and the fingers of the second hand; stop on the fingertips. What did you do this **WEEK**?

Sign Synonym Phrases for **WEEK**: all week, one week

16

Using the 16 handshape also signs the words **SIXTEEN MONTHS** by signing the number 16 and seeing the new month's picture on your calendar. The first hand shows the number **16**. Then, sign **MONTHS** as both hands take the handshape of 1. Crisscross the fingers and place the first finger of the first hand, with the palm facing the body, behind the first finger of the second hand. Touch the first hand's finger to the fingernail of the second hand's first finger. Slide the finger of the first hand down to the base of the first finger of the second hand. Which **MONTH** is your birthday?

Sign Synonym & Phrase for **MONTH**: one month, rent

The hand creates part one of the handshape for **17** as the third finger bends down to touch the thumb and the first, second and fourth fingers point up and apart. Then, for part two, twist the hand at the wrist toward the side and to the front. End with the palm facing the front.

Visualize the words **SEVENTEEN THOUSAND** by signing the number 17 and showing the comma and the three zeros needed to write **17,000**. The first hand signs the number **17**. Then, sign **THOUSAND** by changing the shape of the first hand to Flat 15 with the palm facing the side. The second hand takes the shape of B-L with the palm facing the opposite side. Touch the first hand's fingertips on the palm of the second hand.

Sign Synonym Phrase for **THOUSAND**: one thousand

17

Using the 17 handshape also signs the words **SEVENTEEN YEARS** by signing the number 17 and showing a year as a rotation of the earth once around the sun.

The first hand shows the number **17**. Then, sign **YEARS** as both hands take the shape of S with the palms facing the body. Place the forearm of the second hand horizontally in front of the body. Place the first hand on top of the second hand. Rotate the first hand on top of the second hand forward and down in a circle around the second hand. Both hands end up back in their original position. What **YEAR** did you graduate?

Sign Synonym Phrases for **YEAR**: one year, a year

The hand creates part one of the handshape for **18** as the middle finger bends down to touch the thumb and the first, third and last fingers point up and apart. Then, for part two, twist the hand at the wrist forward toward the side and to the front. End with the palm facing the front.

Visualize the words **EIGHTEEN MILLION** by signing the number 18 and showing the two commas and the zeros needed to write **18,000,000**. The first hand shows the number **18**. Then, sign **MILLION** by changing the shape of the first hand to Flat 15 with the palm facing the side. The second hand takes the shape of B-L with the palm facing the opposite side. Tap the fingertips of the first hand on the palm of the second hand. Then, move the first hand up a bit and tap on the second hand's fingers with the first hand.

Sign Synonym for **MILLION**: millionaire

18

Using the 18 handshape also signs the words **EIGHTEEN INCHES** by signing the number 18 and showing the exact measurement.

The first hand signs the number **18**. Then, sign **INCHES** with both hands taking the shape of Y with both palms facing the front. Place both hands comfortably in front of the body side by side with the thumbs only a short distance apart. Tap the thumbs together a few times.

Sign Synonyms for **INCH**: measure, measurement

The hand creates part one of the handshape for **19** as the first finger curves down to meet the thumb and the last three fingers point up and apart. Then, for part two, twist the hand at the wrist toward the side and to the front. End with the palm facing the front.

Visualize the word **FREE** as becoming free after your hands had been tied together. Both hands take the shape of F with the palms facing the chest. Place the wrist of the first hand behind the wrist of the second hand. Move both hands out in the opposite direction sideways leaving the palms face the front.

Sign Synonyms: carefree, freedom

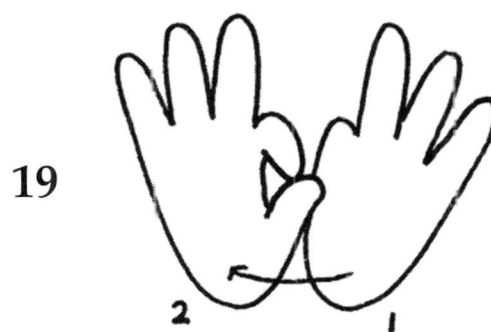

Using the 19 handshape also signs the word **IMPORTANT** as giving someone or something higher significance than others of its kind. Both hands take the shape of 19. With both forearms comfortably at the waist, the palms face up. Touch the last fingers together. Twist the wrists to move the hands apart and up in a small arch. This arch ends with the palms facing down and the first fingers and thumbs touching each other.

Sign Synonyms: appraisal, appraise, esteem, importance, invaluable, meaningful, priceless, significance, significant, valuable, value, worth, worthwhile, worthy

 The hand creates part one of the handshape for **20** as the first finger is parallel to the thumb while the last three fingers fold down to the palm. Then, for part two, tap the first finger on the thumb a few times.

Visualize the word **BIRD** by showing his pointed beak.

The first hand takes the shape of 20 placing the back of the hand on the mouth with the first finger and thumb facing out. Tap the first finger to the thumb a few times.

Sign Synonyms: birds, chicken, fowl

20

Using the 20 handshape also signs the word **PRINT** as pressing the ink onto paper.

The first hand takes the shape of 20 with the finger and thumb facing out and the second hand takes the shape of B-L with the palm facing up. Place the first hand's thumb at the base of palm of the second hand. Tap the first finger on the thumb.

Sign Synonyms: issue, newspaper, publication, publish

The hand creates part one of the handshape for **21** as the first finger and the thumb point out and apart while the last three fingers fold down to the palm. Then, for part two, bend the thumb down at the knuckle and back up a few times.

Visualize the word **GUN** as if you are pretending to hold a pistol. The first hand takes the shape of 21. With the palm facing the side, wiggle the thumb. Be sure you are not pointing the first finger directly at the person you are talking with but rather pointing off to the side. Do you play with a water **GUN**?

Sign Synonyms: firearm, guns, handgun, revolver

21

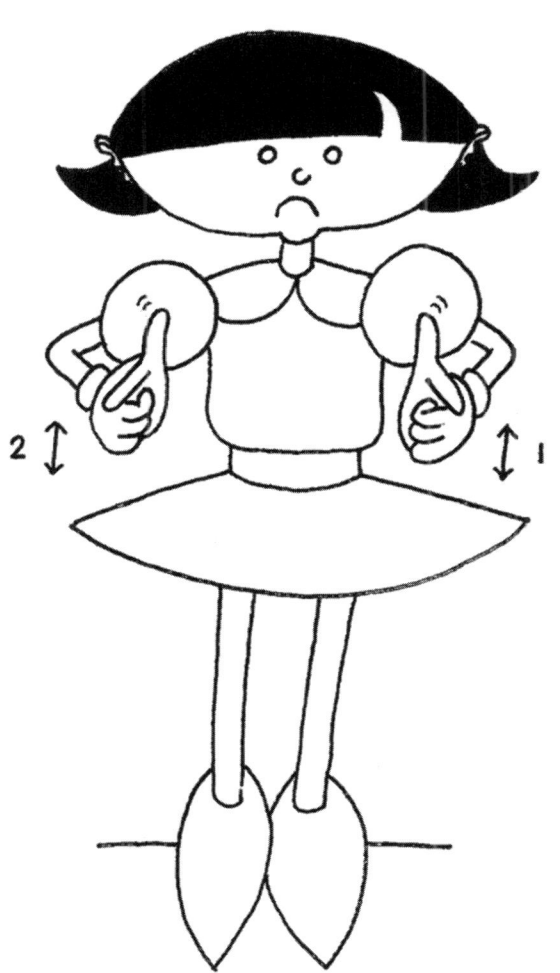

Using the 21 handshape also signs the word **SHOOTOUT** as firing off the guns.

Both hands take the shape of 21 placed in front of the body with the palms facing each other. Wiggle the thumb of the first hand at the same time moving the hand up and down. Then the second hand wiggles the thumb and moving the hand up and down. Repeat the motion a few times.

Sign Synonyms: cowboy, gunfire, gunman, outlaw

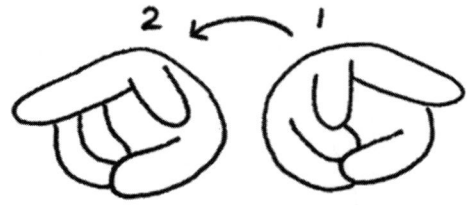

The hand creates part one of the handshape for **22** as the first two fingers point up and apart while the last two fingers fold down to the palm. The thumb rests across the third finger. Tilt the hand forward so the fingers point straight out. Then, for part two, move the wrist in a small arch toward the side, as if bouncing the 2.

Visualize the word **BROWSE** as looking around at the mall to see what is new. As both hands take the shape of 22, place both hands in front of the body with the palms facing forward. Move the hands up and down at the wrists while at the same time gradually moving the hands to the side.

Sign Synonym Phrase: just looking

22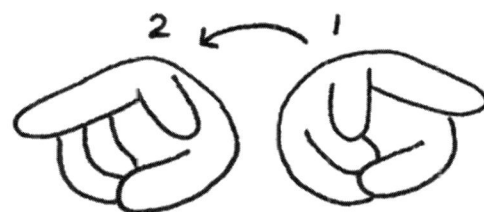

Using the 22 handshape also signs the word **HIGHWAY** showing two lanes of traffic going in opposite directions.

With both hands taking the shape of 22, place the second hand a bit behind the first hand with the palms facing down. At the same time, move the hands in opposite directions so they pass each other. Return each hand to its starting position. Repeat this movement a few times.

Sign Synonyms: freeway, interstate

The hand creates part one of the handshape for **23** as the first finger and the thumb point up and apart and the second finger points forward diagonally. The last two fingers fold down to the palm. Then, for part two, wiggle the middle finger back and forth a few times.

Visualize the word **HURDLE** as a barrier that a person or a horse must leap over during a race.

The first hand takes the shape of 23 with the palm facing down. The second hand takes the shape of 1, its palm also facing down, the first finger points to the side. Place the first hand behind the second hand. Move the first hand forward and across the second hand. During this movement, the first hand's third finger touches and slides over the first finger of the second hand.

23

Using the 23 handshape also signs the words **TWENTY-THREE TIMES** by signing the number 23 and pointing to the wrist as if wearing a watch. The first hand signs the number 23. Then sign **TIMES** by changing the shape of the first hand to Bent 1 with the palm facing down. The second hand takes the shape of B-L. Place the second hand's forearm out in front of the body. The second hand should be comfortably relaxed with its palm facing down. Tap the first finger of the first hand on top of the wrist of the second hand a few times.

Sign Synonyms & Phrases for **TIME**: one time, timed, timing, what time is it?

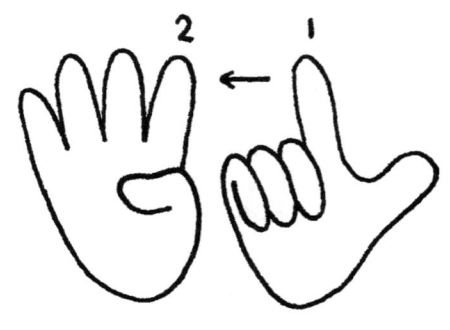

The hand creates part one of the handshape for **24** as the first finger and the thumb point out and apart while the last three fingers fold down to the palm. Then, for part two, move the hand to the side a little bit while changing the handshape to 4.

Visualize the words **TWENTY-FOUR HOURS** by signing the number 24 and showing the big hand making a full circle on the clock. The first hand signs the number **24**. Then, sign **HOURS** with the first hand taking the shape of 1. The second hand takes the shape of B-L. With the palms facing each other, touch the first hand's fingers to the palm of the second hand. Move the first hand directly to the side an inch or so away from the second hand. While the second hand waits in the same position, the first hand moves around in a small circle and lands back in the original position.
Sign Synonym & Phrase for **HOUR**: hourly, one hour

24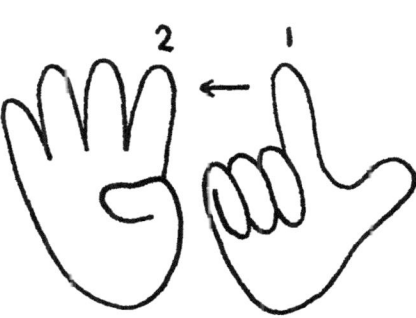

Using the 24 handshape also signs the words **TWENTY-FOUR MINUTES** by signing the number 24 and seeing the minute hand on the clock moving bit by bit.

The first hand signs the number **24**. Then, sign **MINUTES** by changing the shape of the first hand to 1 with the palm facing the second hand. The second hand takes the shape of B-L with the palm facing the first hand. Touch the first hand's fingers on the palm of the second hand. Twist the first hand at the wrist to move it forward a short distance.

Sign Synonym & Phrase for **MINUTE**: moment, one minute

The hand creates part one of the handshape for **25** as the thumb and all the fingers point up and apart. Then move the middle finger forward. Then, for part two, wiggle the middle finger back and forth a few times.

Visualize the phrase **TO TAKE ADVANTAGE OF** as if someone is adding extra things to your bill without asking you first.

The first hand takes the shape of 25 with the palm facing down and the second hand takes the shape of B-L with the palm facing up. Place the first hand's middle finger on the palm of the second hand. Move the first hand back and away from the second hand by sliding the middle finger across the palm of the second hand. The first hand stops a few inches from the second hand in the 5-8 handshape.

Sign Synonyms & Phrase: advantage, exploit, manipulate, rip-off

25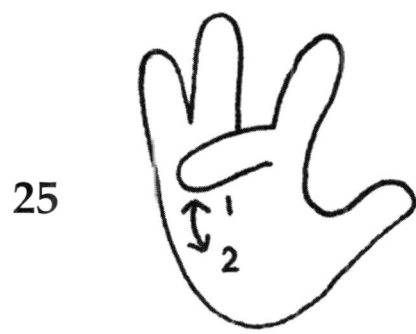

Using the 25 handshape also signs the word **WAIT** as if someone is telling you hold on a minute.

Both hands create the shape of 25 with the palms facing the body. Place the first hand slightly behind the second hand. Wiggle the middle fingers of both hands back and forth. "What are you **WAITING** for? Let's go!"

Sign Synonyms & Phrase: await, hang on, hesitate

REFERENCES

Carmel, S., (1982). *International Hand Alphabet Charts*. Silver Springs, MD: National Association for the Deaf.

Corson, H., & Stuckless, E. (1994). "*Special Programs, Full Inclusion, and Choices for Students Who Are Deaf.*" American Annals of the Deaf, issue 139(2), 148-171.

Costello, E. (1999). *Webster's American Sign Language Dictionary*. New York City, NY: Random House.

Deaf Use Online Interpreter In Aberdeen: KELOLAND News at Ten (2008). CBS TV, January 2008. 22.10 hours. Online version: http://www.keloland.com/NewsDetail6162.cfm?Id=0,65110 [viewed 10/24/08].

Dickinson, L. (2003). *The Use of a Reading Program and Signing to Develop Language Communication Skills in a Toddler with Down Syndrome*. Civitan, issue 85(2), 12-13.
Online version: http://www.loveandlearning.com/lauralee.shtml [viewed 10/10/08].

Glazer, S. (2001). "*Is It a Sign?*" The Washington Post, March 13, 2001, p HE12
Online version: http://www.littlesigners.com/article15.html [viewed 10/03/08].

Gordon, Raymond G., Jr. (2005). *Ethnologue: Languages of the World*. Dallas, TX: SIL International.
Online version: http://www.ethnologue.com/show_language.asp?code=ase [viewed 9/28/08].

Humphries, T. & Padden, C. (1992). *Learning American Sign Language*. Englewood Cliffs, NJ: Prentice Hall.

Indiana School for the Deaf (1995). "*ASL Bill Signed by Governor!*" The Hoosier, issue 1 (17), 1.

Johnson, R., Liddel, S., & Erting, C. (1989). *Unlocking the Curriculum: Principles for Achieving Access in Deaf Education*. Washington, DC: Gallaudet University, Gallaudet Research Institute.

Kannapell, B. (1974). "*Bilingualism: A New Direction In The Education Of The Deaf.*" The Deaf American, issue 9, 15.

Lane, H., Hoffmeister, R., & Bahan, B. (1996). *A Journey into the Deaf-World*. San Diego, CA: Dawn Sign Press.

Lucas, C. (1995). *Sociolinguistics in Deaf Communities*. Washington, D.C.: Gallaudet University Press.

Mayer, C. & Akamatsu, T. (1999). "Bilingual-Bicultural Models of Literacy Education for Deaf Students: Considering the Claims." Journal of Deaf Studies and Deaf Education, issue 4(1), 1-8.

Mirenda, P. (2003). "Toward Functional Augmentative and Alternative Communication for Students With Autism: Manual signs, graphic symbols, and voice output communication aids." Language, Speech, and Hearing Services in Schools, issue 34, 203-216.

Nover, S. (1993). "Who will shape the future of Deaf education?" The Deaf American, issue 43, 117-123.

Seton, E. (2000). *Sign Talk of the Cheyenne Indians*. Mineola, NY: Dover Publications, Inc.

Smith, C., Lentz, E., & Mikos, K. (1988). *Signing Naturally*. San Diego, CA: Dawn Sign Press.

Strong, M. (1995). "A Review of Bilingual / Bicultural Programs for Deaf children in North America." American Annals of the Deaf, issue 140(2), 84-94.

Tucker, J. (1995). "1893, 1993, and "MSD has come full circle…" The Maryland Bulletin, issue 116(1), 13. Online version: http://www.msd.edu/media/mdb/mdbarchives/v116i1_1995_fall.pdf [viewed 11/08/08].

Valli, C. (1995). *ASL Poetry: Selected Works of Clayton Valli*. San Diego, CA: Dawn Sign Press. DVD.

Wilcox, S. & Peyton, J. (1998). "American Sign Language as a Foreign Language." The ERIC Review, issue 6(1). Online version: http://www.accesseric.org/resources/ericreview/vol6no1/asl.html [viewed 10/17/08].

INDEX

A

A, 12-13
Open A, 14-15
a case of, 165
a group of, 25
a lot, 82
ability, 31
able, 31
abolish, 114
abort, 114
accuracy, 112
accurate, 112
act, 12
adept, 31
advance, 195
advanced, 195
advancement, 195
advantage, 214
agile, 31
airline, 61
airplane, 61
airport, 61
album, 19
all day, 166
all week, 196
allowance, 111
alternate, 66
altogether, 13
amaze, 47
amazement, 47
America, 150
American, 150
anniversary, 109
annual, 184
anthem, 154
appear, 21
appraisal, 203
appraise, 203
appreciate, 155
appreciation, 155
army, 14
art, 58
assortment, 119
astound, 47
attach, 39
attachment, 39
attention, 17
avenge, 113
await, 215

B

B, 16-17
B-L, 18-19
B-L-1, 20-21
B-L-U, 22-23
back out, 55
ballet, 101
band, 154
battery, 130
be careful, 64
begin, 20
belong, 39
best, 192
better, 192
bewildered, 47
bind, 39
binoculars, 76
bird(s), 204
bond, 39
bone, 102
book, 19
booklet, 19
books, 19
borrow, 139
boss, 27
box, 165
boy, 28
bracket(s), 25
bronco, 189
browse, 208
butterfly, 193

C

C, 24-25
Wide C, 26-27
Flat C, 28-29
C-L, 30-31
cage, 146
California, 60
calm, 16
calm down, 16
camera, 43
capable, 31
camp, 133
camping, 133
can(s), 164
captain, 27
card, 44
carefree, 202
careful, 64
cat, 177
category, 25
cautious, 64
celebrate, 109
celebration, 109
ceremony, 109

champagne, 115
champion, 143
championship, 143
chapel, 24
charge, 131
charity, 106
check, 44
chicken, 204
chief, 27
choice, 38
choir, 154
choose, 38
chuckle, 67
church, 24
class, 25
classify, 25
clown, 81
college, 18
collegiate, 18
colt, 189
combat, 14
combination, 183
combine, 183
compatible, 183
compatibility, 183
competition, 181
composition, 46
concert, 154
concise, 112
connect, 39
connection, 39
consolidate, 183
contest, 181
contribution, 106
cost, 131
costly, 126
coupon, 44
cowboy, 207
cry out, 153
cup, 164
current, 117

cute, 188

D

D, 32-33
dance, 101
date, 32
dating, 32
day(s), 166
daytime, 166
define, 174
definition, 174
delete, 114
describe, 174
description, 174
dessert, 32
devout, 56
diamond, 33
difficult, 103
dine, 127
dirt, 85
disco, 101
diversity, 119
doctor, 70
dollar(s), 169
donate, 106
donation, 106
donkey, 191
double, 138
drama, 12
draw back, 55
drawing, 58
drop out, 55
drum, 108
dusk, 167

E

E, 34-35

eat, 127
economic, 35
economy, 35
edit, 46
educate, 78
education, 78
efficient, 31
eight dollars, 169
eight hundred, 168
eighteen inches, 201
eighteen million, 200
eighth, 169
electric, 130
electricity, 130
elevate, 195
elevated, 195
eliminate, 114
enable, 31
energetic, 34
energy, 34
engine, 182
English, 30
enjoy, 155
envelope, 44
esteem, 203
evening, 167
every year, 184
exact, 112
exactly, 112
exalt, 195
exalted, 195
expensive, 126
experience, 149
expert, 31
explain, 174
explanation, 174
exploit, 214
eye-popping, 80

F

F, 36-37
Open F, 38-39
factory, 182
faith, 175
faithful, 175
fare, 131
fee, 131
feel, 160
feelings, 160
fence, 147
festival, 109
few, 84
fight back, 113
file, 22
filly, 189
find, 176
fine, 131
firearm, 206
fit in, 183
five-fold, 156
folk, 86
food, 127
forest(s), 151
fortunate, 161
fortune, 26
found, 176
fowl, 204
fox, 178
free, 202
freedom, 202
freeway, 209
freshman, 158
frog, 187

G

G, 40-41
Curvy G, 42-43
Wide G, 44-45
Closed G, 46-47
G-H, 48-49
Curvy G-H, 50-51
gala, 101
Gallaudet, 40
Gallaudet University, 40
garage, 141
general, 27
get even, 113
ghost, 37
gift, 106
gift box, 165
giving, 106
giggle, 67
girl, 180
glass, 164
go by train, 98
going out with, 32
gold, 60
golden, 60
graduation, 41
grant, 106
ground, 85
growl, 153
guide, 29
guidance, 29
gunfire, 207
gunman, 207
gun(s), 206

H

H, 52-53
Bent H, 54-55
H-Y, 56-57
handgun, 206
handy, 31
hang on, 215
harmony, 154
hesitate, 215
higher, 195
highest, 195
highness, 52
highway, 209
holy, 56
Holy Spirit, 36
honor, 52
honorable, 52
horse, 188
hurdle, 210
hour(s), 212
hourly, 212
hundred, 168
hymn, 154

I

I, 58-59
I-L-Y, 60-61
I feel, 160
I have an idea, 59
I have no, 124
idea, 59
illustration, 58
importance, 203
important, 203
in good standing, 56
inch(es), 201
incident, 21
indoctrinate, 78
indoctrination, 78
industry, 182
instruct, 78
instruction, 78
interstate, 209
invaluable, 203
is called, 53
issue, 205

J

J, 62-63
jackpot, 26
jail, 146
jam, 62
jelly, 62
jet, 61
journey, 136
juice, 63
junior, 163

K

K, 64-65
kid, 132
kids, 132
kitchen, 65

L

L, 66-67
land, 85
laugh, 67
laughing, 67
laughter, 67
lead, 29
leader, 29
learn, 148
learned, 148
learning, 148
leisure, 155
lend me, 139
light, 172
lightning, 118
like, 170
limousine, 51
lots, 82
luck, 161
lucky, 161

M

M, 68-69
Open M, 70-71
machine, 182
manipulate, 214
manufacture, 182
many, 82
many pluses, 129
mare, 189
match, 183
materialize, 21
mature, 69
maturity, 69
McDonald's ®, 68
meaningful, 203
measure, 201
measurement, 201
medical doctor, 70
melody, 154
melon, 173
memorable, 71
memorial, 71
Memorial Day, 71
mental, 128
merge, 183
message, 171
microwave, 83
microwave oven, 83
midnight, 186
military, 14
million, 200
millionaire, 200
mind, 128
minute(s), 213
modern, 117
moment, 213
month(s), 197
moon, 42
morals, 69
more, 79
motor, 182
mule, 191
multitude, 82
music, 154
musical, 154
mustang, 189

N

N, 72-73
Open N, 74-75
name, 53
nation, 74
national, 74
natural, 74
nature, 74
necessary, 107
need, 107
nephew, 73
new idea, 59
newspaper, 205
next, 66
nickel, 162
niece, 73
niece and nephew, 73
night(s), 167
no, 48
no way, 48
nobody, 124
nominee, 53
none, 124
none of that, 124
nope, 48
normal, 74
north, 72
northern, 72
not following the rules, 57

note, 171
nothing, 124
numerous, 82
nurse, 75
nursing, 75

O

O, 76-77
Oval O, 78-79
Wide O, 80-81
O-S, 82-83
Wavy O, 84-85
occur, 21
of course, 74
officer, 27
omit, 114
one hour, 212
one minute, 213
one month, 197
one time, 211
one thousand, 198
one week, 196
one year, 199
opinion, 125
opportunity, 77
optimism, 129
ordeal, 149
origin, 20
outlaw, 207
owl, 76
owlet, 76

P

P, 86-87
package(s), 165
paper clip, 49
park, 140

party, 116
passive, 16
pastor, 37
pay attention, 17
pension, 111
people, 86
performance, 12
perspective, 100
photograph, 43
photography, 43
physician, 70
pick up, 176
Pierre (South Dakota), 87
pious, 56
pitch, 142
pitcher, 142
plane, 61
play, 116
pleasure, 155
point of view, 100
political, 87
politician, 87
politics, 87
pony, 189
pop up, 21
popcorn, 185
population, 86
positive, 129
pound, 99
power, 130
practice, 15
preach, 37
precise, 112
preparatory, 157
present, 117, 165
price, 131
priceless, 203
print, 205
prison, 146
privacy fence, 147
problem, 103

proficient, 31
prominent, 195
promote, 195
promotion, 195
property, 85
publication, 205
publish, 205
pumpkin, 173

Q

Q, 88-89
qualification, 89
qualify, 89
quality, 89
queen, 88
quiet, 16
quit, 55

R

R, 90-91
R-L, 92-93
race, 181
railroad, 98
rehearsal, 15
reject, 114
remove, 114
rent, 197
repel, 114
research, 91
resign, 55
restart, 20
retaliate, 113
retire, 93
retirement, 93
revenge, 113
review, 92
revolver, 206

223

rich, 26
rid, 114
ride, 50
riding, 50
righteous, 56
ring, 159
ring finger, 159
rip-off, 214
roar, 153
rocket, 90
romp, 116
room, 165
royalty, 111

S

S, 94-95
scale, 99
scream, 153
section, 25
see, 134
select, 38
senate, 95
senator, 95
sensation, 160
sense, 160
series, 25
seven days, 166
seven nights, 167
seventeen thousand, 198
seventeen years, 199
several, 84
shock, 47
shootout, 207
should, 107
shout, 153
show, 12
show up, 21
sight, 134
significance, 203

significant, 203
silence, 16
silent, 16
sing, 154
sit, 54
sit down, 54
six cans, 164
six packages, 165
sixteen months, 197
sixteen weeks, 196
sketch, 58
skill, 31
skilled, 31
skit, 12
skyrocket, 90
snapshot, 43
soil, 85
soldier, 14
song, 154
sort, 22
space rocket, 90
spirit, 37
spiritual, 37
sport, 181
spot, 179
stain, 179
stallion, 189
standpoint, 100
start, 20
start off, 45
startle, 47
still, 16
subscribe, 111
subscription, 111
supposed to, 107
surface, 21
surprise, 47

T

T, 96-97
take care, 64
talent, 31
tax, 131
teach, 78
team, 96
tent, 133
terminate, 114
textbook, 19
theater, 12
there is nothing (for), 124
think, 128
third, 145
thought, 128
thousand, 198
through, 23
ticket, 137
tiger, 152
time(s), 211
timed, 211
timing, 211
to pick one, 38
to ride with, 50
to take advantage of, 214
toad, 187
today, 117, 166
together, 13
toll, 131
tonight, 167
tour, 136
train, 98
training, 15
tranquil, 16
transfer, 136
travel, 136
travel by train, 98
treasure, 26
tree(s), 151
tribute, 106

trip, 136
triple, 144
trouble, 190
troublesome, 190
Tuesday, 97
turn, 66
turn up, 21
twenty-four hours, 212
twenty-four minutes, 213
twenty-three times, 211
twice, 138

U

U, 98-99
uh-huh, 94
unholiness, 57
unite, 39
unrighteous, 57
upright, 56
urgent, 117

V

V, 100-101
Bent V, 102-103
valuable, 203
value, 203
variety, 119
various, 119
vengeance, 113
via, 23
viewpoint, 100
visualize, 134
vocal, 135
voice, 135
volume, 135

W

W, 104-105
wait, 215
waltz, 101
water, 104
wealth, 26
week(s), 196
weigh, 99
weight, 99
welfare, 111
what time is it?, 211
who, 110
whom, 110
whose, 110
with, 13
woods, 151
world, 105
worth, 203
worthwhile, 203
worthy, 203
write, 46

X

X, 106-107
X-A, 108-109
X-L, 110-111
X-O, 112-113
X-T, 114-115
xylophone, 108

Y

Y, 116-117
yeah, 94
year(s), 199
yell, 153
yes, 94

young, 194
younger, 194
youth, 194
yup, 94

Z

Z, 118-119
zoom, 45

NUMBERS

Zero, 124-125
Oval Zero, 126-127

1, 128-129
Bent 1, 130-131
1-I, 132-133

2, 134-135
Bent 2, 136-137
2-K, 138-139

3, 140-141
Bent 3, 142-143
3-K, 144-145

4, 146-147
Open 4, 148-149

5, 150-151
Bent 5, 152-153
Closed 5, 154-155

5-6, 156-157
5-7, 158-159
5-8, 160-161
5-9, 162-163

6, 164-165

7, 166-167

8, 168-169
Open 8, 170-171
8-S, 172-173

9, 174-175
Open 9, 176-177
9-S, 178-179

10, 180-181
Wide 10, 182-183

11, 184-185

12, 186-187

13, 188-189

14, 190-191

15, 192-193
Flat 15, 194-195

16, 196-197

17, 198-199

18, 200-201

19, 202-203

20, 204-205

21, 206-207

22, 208-209

23, 210-211

24, 212-213

25, 214-215

For those of you who have terrific talent or superb skills, your dreams can come true as well. If you want to become a model, a musician, an artist, a writer (of poems, books, or films), a producer, or a filmmaker, please review the information at our website: www.GiordanoEntertainment.com. For information regarding book signing, tour locations, large quantity discounts, promotion, and advertising, contact Giordano World Entertainment. ™

Giordano World Entertainment ™
Angelo Giordano
Four Turnberry Place Suite 1905
2777 Paradise Road
Las Vegas, NV 89109

www.GiordanoEntertainment.com